Teacher Guide Level C

STECK-VAUGHN

SUMMER

STUDIO

MATH

Steck
Vaughn™

A Harcourt Achieve Imprint

www.Steck-Vaughn.com
1-800-531-5015

Contents

Lessons

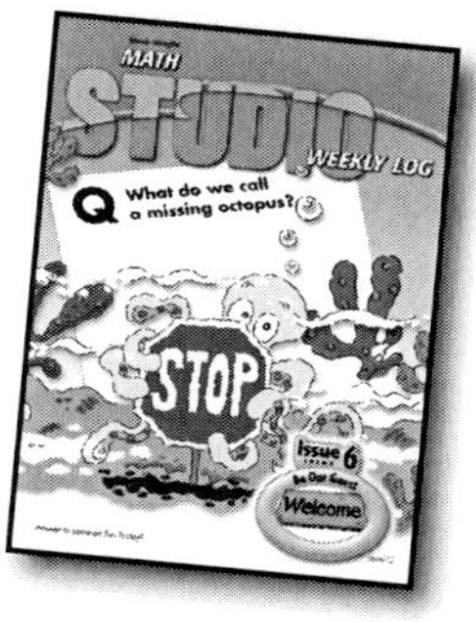

Blackline Masters 62

Fact Fluencies, Pre-Test, Weekly Assessment,
Cumulative Assessment, Manipulatives,
Projects, Worksheets

Motivate

Summer Studio Math builds students' confidence to tackle new problems and to learn new skills. You will know students feel empowered when they say,

Accelerate

Build **foundational understandings** to accelerate students' learning

Number Sense	**Meanings of Operations**	**Fact Fluency**	**Problem Solving**
• Understands place-value structure • Can decompose numbers • Represents numbers in different ways • Makes reasonable estimates • Can judge reasonableness of answers	• Knows when to add, subtract, multiply or divide • Understands how operations relate to one another	• Uses strategies to learn facts • Develops automaticity	• Builds mathematical knowledge • Applies a variety of strategies • Participates in mathematical conversations • Develops a positive disposition towards mathematics

Clear and Easy-to-follow

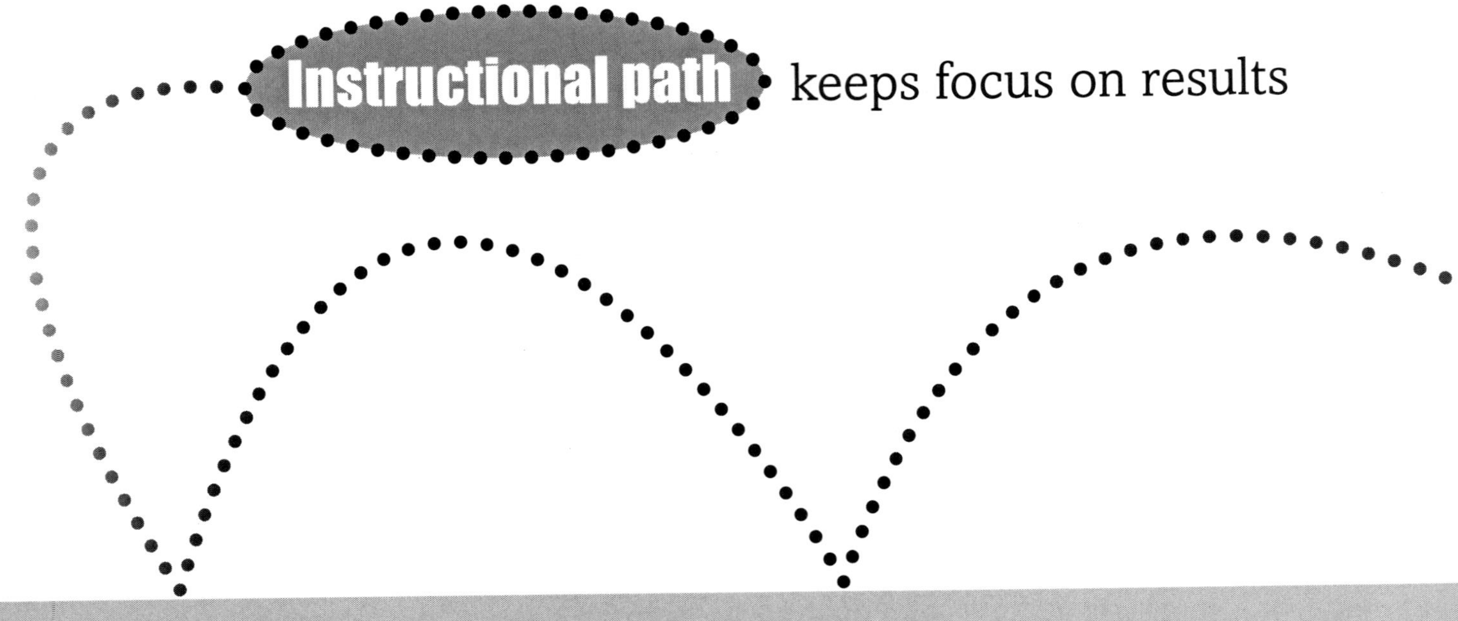

Instructional path keeps focus on results

Assess

- Identify what students know and are able to do.

- Use the pre-test to inform instruction.

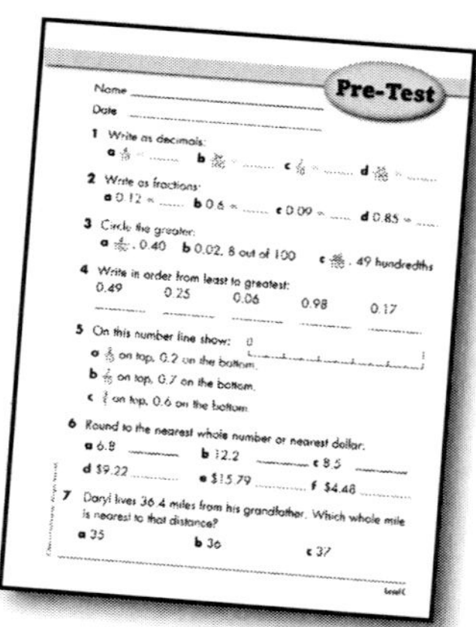

Teach

Make sense of mathematical concepts through
- mathematical conversations
- using manipulatives
- modeling
- explaining
- making connections
- justifying answers

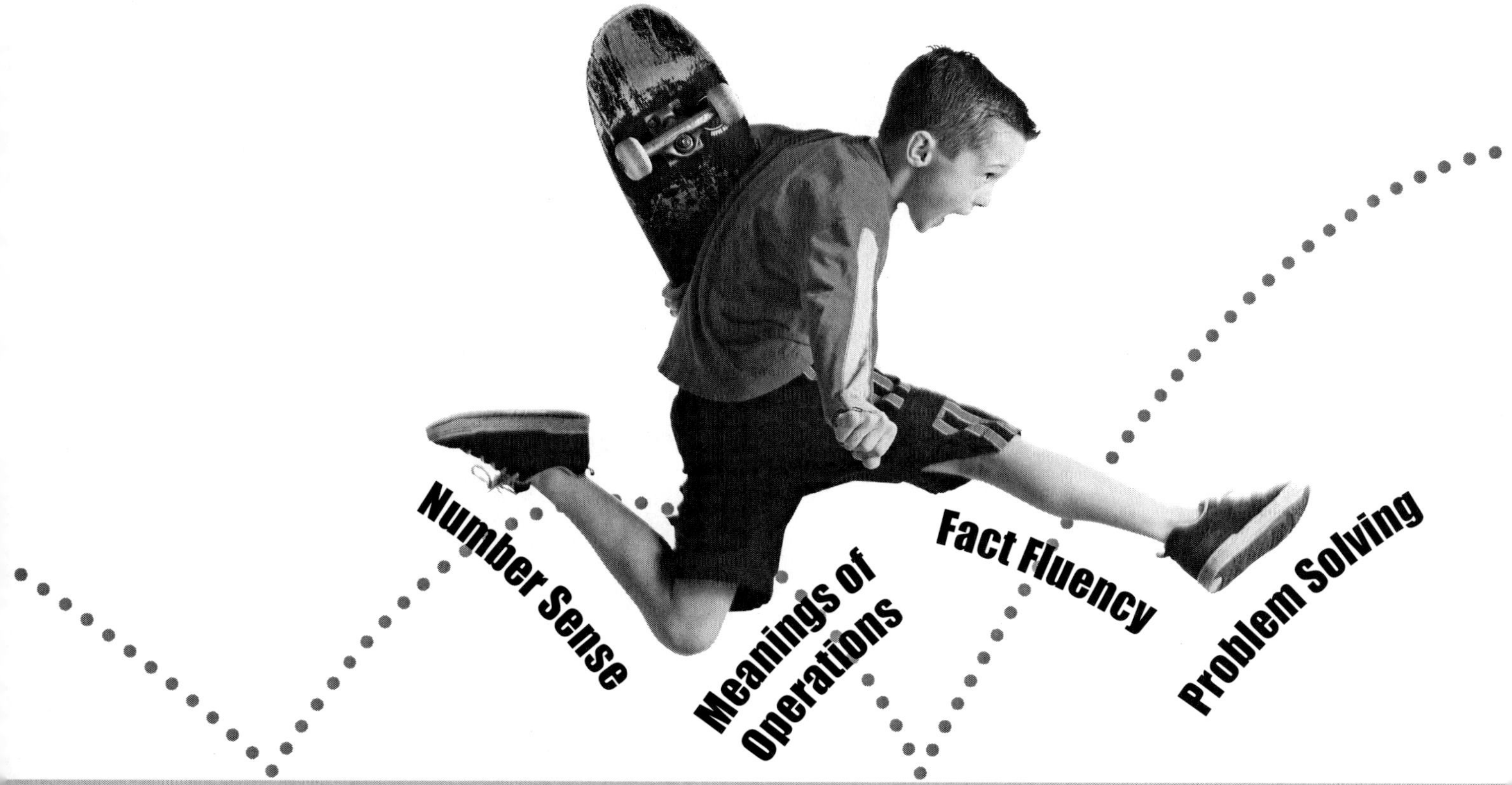

Reteach

- Identify students who would benefit from reteaching and additional practice through weekly assessment.

- Reteach individuals or small groups while the rest of the class is working on their Studio Weekly Logs.

Results

- Document higher levels of achievement with a midpoint cumulative and endpoint summative assessments.

- Celebrate success with reward cards

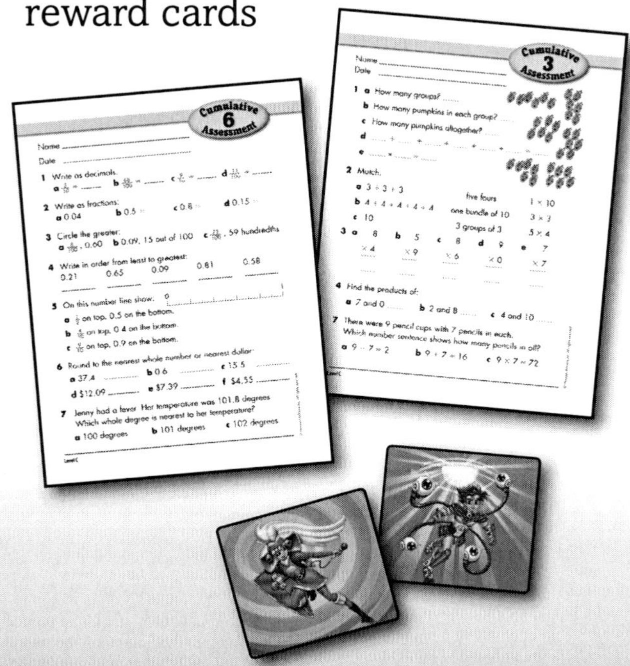

Assess for Achievement

Summer Studio Math assessment
- Provides information to the teacher for making instructional decisions
- Provides meaningful information to the student about his/her own learning
- Documents cumulative learning at midpoint and end of program

Assessment Tools

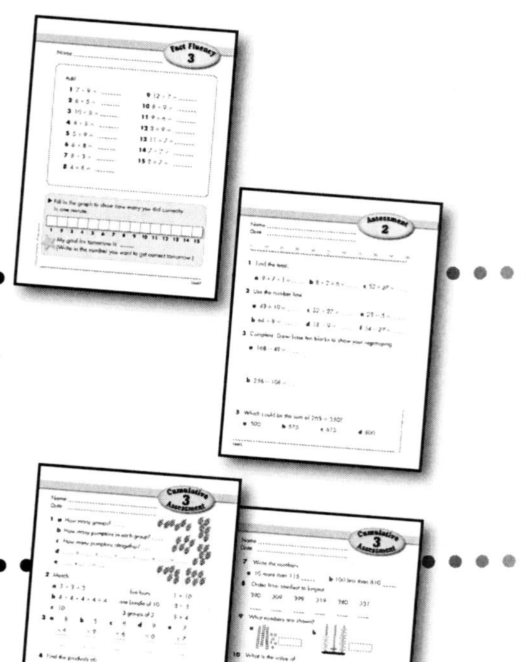

Pre-test
- Documents strengths and weaknesses
- Establishes a baseline of students' skills

Daily fact fluency
- Mental math and fact assessment
- Students monitor their own progress
- Encourage goal setting

Weekly written assessments
- Inform instruction
- Alert need for reteaching
- Monitor progress

Cumulative assessment
- Midpoint alert for reteaching
- Document midpoint achievement

Post-test
- Document student progress
- Evaluate against national standards
- Inform instruction for next year's teacher

Flexible Use

Summer Studio Math can be customized to meet your needs.

4-Week Plan	6-Week Plan	8-Week Plan

- Choose four weeks from among the six weekly lesson plans based on student pretest needs as presented.

- Use all weeks

- Add one or two extra days for projects to all instructional weeks.

  or

- Add extra days for practice before or after assessments.

Six Instructional Levels

Level	Recommended Use
Level A	Grade 1
Level B	Grade 2
Level C	Grade 3
Level D	Grade 4
Level E	Grade 5
Level F	Grade 6

Themes match Summer Studio Reading

An All-in-One Solution

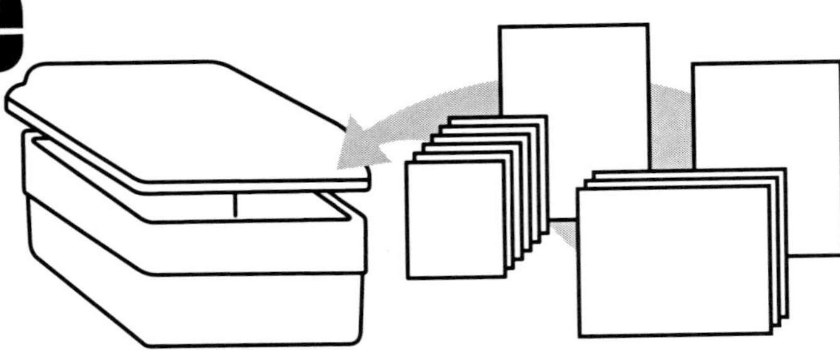

Studio Weekly Log

- Six colorful take-home books—one for each week
- Provide daily practice of the week's math skills
- Recording form for the Activity Cards that students complete
- A place for students to tell their families what math they learned that week

Reward Cards

- A new super-cool card for each student each week
- Collectible and fun
- Funny math riddles on one side and Summer Studio superheroes on the other
- Double the fun with *Summer Studio Reading* rewards cards – same superheroes; different jokes

Manipulatives

- Provide teacher and students with tools to model concepts
- Help students develop understandings of the big ideas in mathematics
- Everything needed to teach the lessons is included in the kit

Teacher's Guide

- Clear easy-to-follow 8-step lessons
- Blackline masters for fact fluency, games, workmats, assessments, award certificates, and weekly projects
- Answer keys
- Preparation lists for each day
- NCTM standards for every lesson

Concept Posters

- A new poster each week
- Supports instruction
- Serves as a reference of the big math ideas

Activity Cards

- Provide extra practice
- Motivate with fun activities
- Provide opportunities to review and practice math from other strands—algebra, data analysis, probability, geometry, and measurement

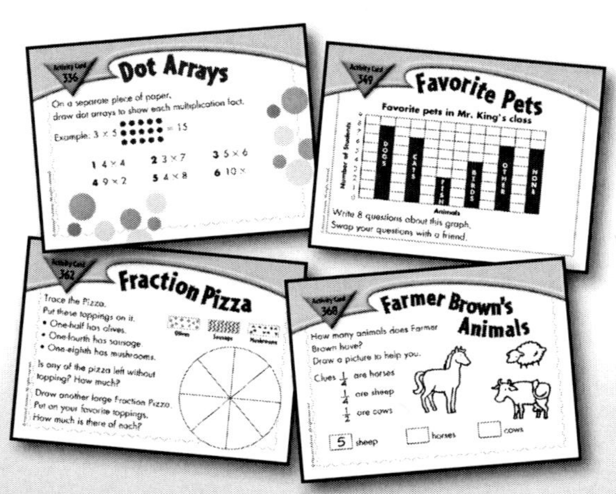

Teacher Lessons Provide Clear Navigation—Each Week, Each Day

Daily fact practice

At a glance skills that will be taught in this lesson

Everything needed to teach the lesson

Standards for every lesson

Clear easy-to-follow plan for instruction

Essential question focuses on the big idea

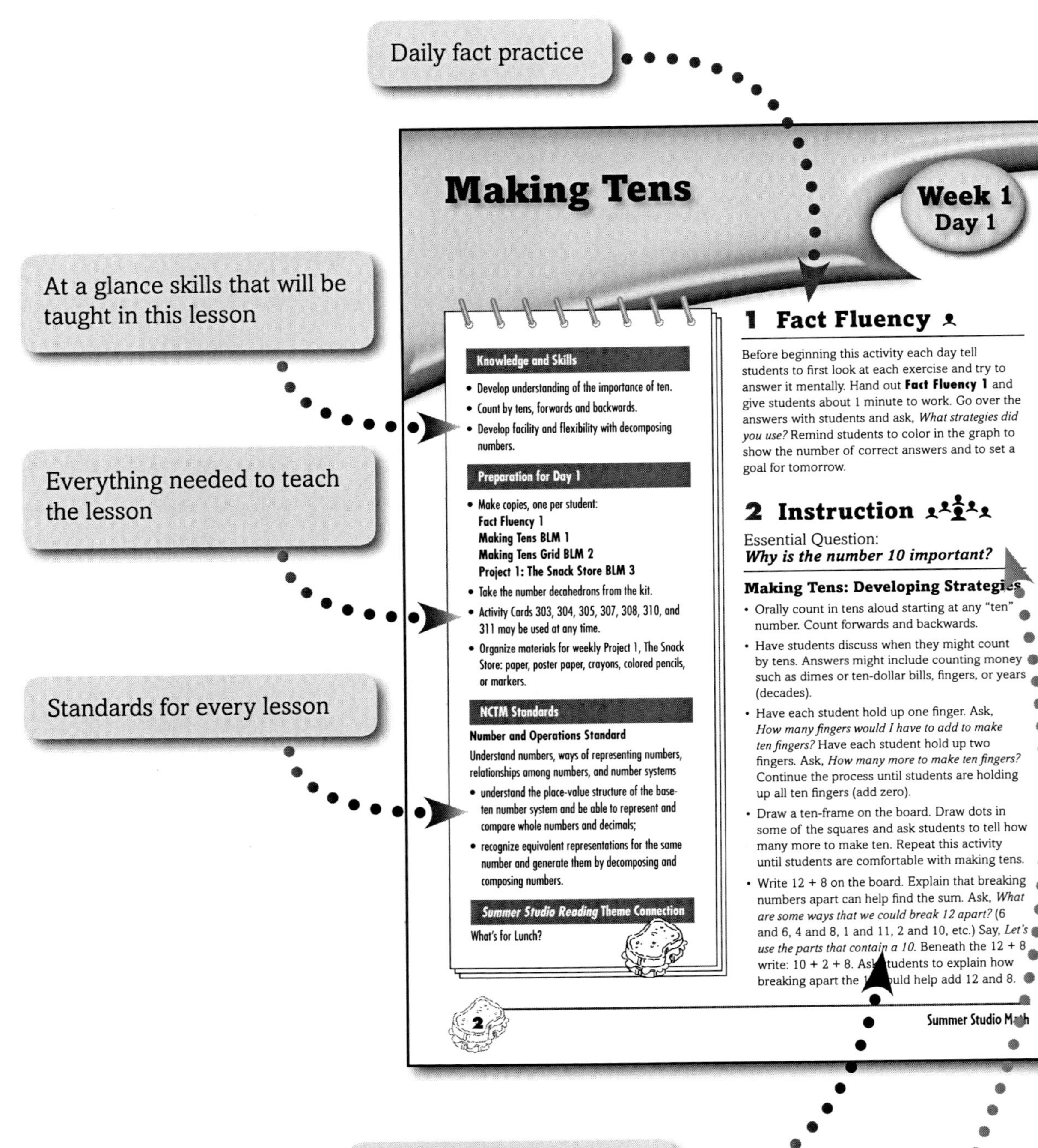

Say, *8 makes ten. 10 + 10 equals 20, so 12 + 8 equals 20.*

- Have students use a similar strategy for 17 + 3, 11 + 9, and 14 + 6.
- Hand out copies of **Making Tens BLM 1**. Have students complete the worksheet and then discuss it as a class.

3 Kinesthetics

Buzz!

- Have students stand around the perimeter of the room and do a few warm-up stretches.
- Say, *Everyone will run in place while we count off around the room. When you get to a number that is a ten, such as ten, twenty, or thirty, say "buzz" instead of the number. For example, 6, 7, 8, 9, "buzz."* Do this for several minutes.

4 Studio Weekly Log

- Have each student work with a partner to complete page 1 of the **Studio Weekly Log**.
- Early Finishers: Provide appropriate **Activity Cards**.

5 Conversation

Have students check to see if each of their answers is reasonable. Then go over the answers together allowing students to share solution strategies and ask questions.

6 Math Game

Making Tens

Play in groups of 3 or 4. Give each student a copy of **Making Tens Grid BLM 2**. Players take turns tossing a number decahedron with numbers 0–9. The number each player tosses must be written into the grid. Rows must add to 10. If a number is tossed that cannot be written in the grid, that

student must wait for his/her next turn to toss again. Whoever completes their grid first, wins.

7 Activity Cards

Provide appropriate cards for students to choose and complete. Remind students to record the number of completed cards in the inside front cover of his/her **Studio Weekly Log**.

8 Weekly Project

- Together read the directions for **Project 1: The Snack Store**.
- Ask students to explain what makes a snack a healthy snack.

Week 1

3

Scope and Sequence
Correlations to NCTM Standards

	Level A	Level B	Level C	Level D	Level E	Level F
Number and Operations Standard						
Understand numbers, ways of representing numbers, relationships among numbers, and number systems	•	•	•	•	•	•
Place-value structure with whole numbers	•	•	•	•	•	•
Place-value structure with decimals			•	•	•	•
Relate, compose, and decompose whole numbers	•	•	•	•	•	•
Generate equivalent representations of numbers by decomposing and composing		•	•	•	•	•
Represent commonly used fractions	•	•	•	•	•	•
Know fractions as parts of wholes and parts of collections		•	•	•	•	•
Recognize fractions as locations on number lines			•	•	•	•
Recognize fractions as divisions of whole numbers				•	•	•
Use benchmarks to judge size of fractions		•	•	•	•	•
Develop meaning of percent					•	•
Compare and order fractions, decimals, and percents					•	•
Read and write large numbers			•	•	•	•
Understand meanings of operations and how they relate to one another	•	•	•	•	•	•
Understands meanings of addition and subtraction of whole numbers	•	•	•	•	•	•
Understands the effects of adding and subtracting whole numbers	•	•	•	•	•	•
Understands situations that entail multiplication and division		•	•	•	•	•

	Level A	Level B	Level C	Level D	Level E	Level F
Understands meanings of multiplication and division		●	●	●	●	●
Understands the effects of multiplying and dividing		●	●	●	●	●
Understands the relationship between operations (as inverses)			●	●	●	●
Understands and uses properties of operations	●	●	●	●	●	●
Understands the meaning and effects of operations with fractions and decimals				●	●	●
Uses commutative property of addition	●	●	●	●	●	●
Uses commutative property of multiplication		●	●	●	●	●
Uses associative and commutative properties of addition and multiplication to simplify computations			●	●	●	●
Compute fluently and make reasonable estimates	●	●	●	●	●	●
Use strategies for whole-number computations	●	●	●	●	●	●
Develop fluency with addition and subtraction	●	●	●	●	●	●
Use a variety of methods to compute including mental computation, estimation, paper and pencil, and using objects for whole numbers	●	●	●	●	●	●
Use a variety of methods to compute including mental computation, estimation, paper and pencil for fractions and decimals				●	●	●
Develop fluency with multiplication and division with basic number combinations		●	●	●	●	●
Use strategies to estimate whole-number computations and to judge reasonableness of answers	●	●	●	●	●	●
Use strategies to estimate computations with fractions and decimals				●	●	●
Use visual models, benchmarks, and equivalent forms to add and subtract commonly used fractions and decimals				●	●	●

	Level A	Level B	Level C	Level D	Level E	Level F
Algebra Standard						
Understand patterns, relations, and functions	●	●	●	●	●	●
Represent and analyze mathematical situations and structures using algebraic symbols	●	●	●	●	●	●
Use mathematical models to represent and understand quantitative relationships	●	●	●	●	●	●
Measurement Standard						
Understand measurable attributes of objects and the units, systems, and processes of measurement	●	●	●	●	●	●
Apply appropriate techniques, tools, and formulas to determine measurements	●	●	●	●	●	●
Data Analysis and Probability Standard						
Formulate questions that can be addressed with data and collect, organize, and display relevant data to answer them	●	●	●	●	●	●
Select and use appropriate statistical methods to analyze data	●	●	●	●	●	●
Develop and evaluate inferences and predictions that are based on data	●	●	●	●	●	●
Problem Solving Standard						
Build new mathematical knowledge through problem solving	●	●	●	●	●	●
Solve problems that arise in mathematics and in other contexts	●	●	●	●	●	●
Apply and adapt a variety of appropriate strategies to solve problems	●	●	●	●	●	●
Monitor and reflect on the process of mathematical problem solving	●	●	●	●	●	●
Communication Standard						
Organize and consolidate their mathematical thinking through communication	●	●	●	●	●	●
Communicate their mathematical thinking coherently and clearly to peers, teachers, and others	●	●	●	●	●	●

	Level A	Level B	Level C	Level D	Level E	Level F
Analyze and evaluate the mathematical thinking and strategies of others	•	•	•	•	•	•
Use the language of mathematics to express mathematical ideas precisely	•	•	•	•	•	•

Connections Standard

	Level A	Level B	Level C	Level D	Level E	Level F
Recognize and use connections among mathematical ideas	•	•	•	•	•	•
Understand how mathematical ideas interconnect and build on one another to produce a coherent whole	•	•	•	•	•	•

Representation Standard

	Level A	Level B	Level C	Level D	Level E	Level F
Create and use representations to organize, record, and communicate mathematical ideas	•	•	•	•	•	•
Use representations to model and interpret physical, social, and mathematical phenomena	•	•	•	•	•	•

Making Tens

1 Fact Fluency

Before beginning this activity each day tell students to first look at each exercise and try to answer it mentally. Hand out **Fact Fluency 1** and give students about 1 minute to work. Go over the answers with students and ask, *What strategies did you use?* Remind students to color in the graph to show the number of correct answers and to set a goal for tomorrow.

2 Instruction

Essential Question:
Why is the number 10 important?

Making Tens: Developing Strategies

- Orally count in tens aloud starting at any "ten" number. Count forwards and backwards.

- Have students discuss when they might count by tens. Answers might include counting money such as dimes or ten-dollar bills, fingers, or years (decades).

- Have each student hold up one finger. Ask, *How many fingers would I have to add to make ten fingers?* Have each student hold up two fingers. Ask, *How many more to make ten fingers?* Continue the process until students are holding up all ten fingers (add zero).

- Draw a ten-frame on the board. Draw dots in some of the squares and ask students to tell how many more to make ten. Repeat this activity until students are comfortable with making tens.

- Write 12 + 8 on the board. Explain that breaking numbers apart can help find the sum. Ask, *What are some ways that we could break 12 apart?* (6 and 6, 4 and 8, 1 and 11, 2 and 10, etc.) Say, *Let's use the parts that contain a 10.* Beneath the 12 + 8 write: 10 + 2 + 8. Ask students to explain how breaking apart the 12 could help add 12 and 8.

Say, *8 makes ten. 10 + 10 equals 20, so 12 + 8 equals 20.*

- Have students use a similar strategy for 17 + 3, 11 + 9, and 14 + 6.
- Hand out copies of **Making Tens BLM 1**. Have students complete the worksheet and then discuss it as a class.

3 Kinesthetics

Buzz!

- Have students stand around the perimeter of the room and do a few warm-up stretches.
- Say, *Everyone will run in place while we count off around the room. When you get to a number that is a ten, such as ten, twenty, or thirty, say "buzz" instead of the number. For example, 6, 7, 8, 9, "buzz."* Do this for several minutes.

4 Studio Weekly Log

- Have each student work with a partner to complete page 1 of the **Studio Weekly Log**.
- Early Finishers: Provide appropriate **Activity Cards**.

5 Conversation

Have students check to see if each of their answers is reasonable. Then go over the answers together allowing students to share solution strategies and ask questions.

6 Math Game

Making Tens

Play in groups of 3 or 4. Give each student a copy of **Making Tens Grid BLM 2**. Players take turns tossing a number decahedron with numbers 0–9. The number each player tosses must be written into the grid. Rows must add to 10. If a number is tossed that cannot be written in the grid, that student must wait for his/her next turn to toss again. Whoever completes their grid first, wins.

7 Weekly Project

- Give each student a copy of **Project 1: The Snack Store BLM 3**. Read the directions together.
- Ask students to explain what makes a snack a healthy snack.

8 Activity Cards

Provide appropriate cards for students to choose and complete. Have a few counters, dot cubes, and number decahedrons set aside for card activity. Remind students to record the number of completed cards in the inside front cover of his/her **Studio Weekly Log**.

Finding Place-Values

Knowledge and Skills

- Read and write numbers through 9,999.
- Develop understanding of place value.
- Understand the relative sizes of numbers.

Preparation for Day 2

- Make copies, one per student:
  Fact Fluency 2
  Place-Value Grids BLM 4
- Take the number decahedrons from the kit. (Math Game)
- Gather calculators, if available. (Math Game)
- Display the **Place-Value** poster.
- Provide materials for weekly project.
- **Activity Cards 301, 302, 306,** and **312** are appropriate for this lesson.

NCTM Standards

Number and Operations Standard

Understand numbers, ways of representing numbers, relationships among numbers, and number systems

- understand the place-value structure of the base-ten number system and be able to represent and compare whole numbers and decimals;
- recognize equivalent representations for the same number and generate them by decomposing and composing numbers.

1 Fact Fluency

Hand out **Fact Fluency 2**. Remind students to color in the graph to show the number of correct answers and to set a goal for tomorrow.

2 Instruction

Place Value: Developing Meaning

- Write the number 2,134 on the board. Ask students to break apart the number.

- Ask, *What does the 4 represent?* (4 ones) *What does the 3 represent?* (3 tens) *What does the 1 represent?* (1 hundred) *What does the 2 represent?* (2 thousands)

- Point to the **Place-Value** poster. Tell students that we show ones with a units cube, tens with a rod, hundreds with a flat, and thousands with a thousands cube. The rod holds 10 unit cubes. The flat holds 100 unit cubes. The thousands cube holds 1,000 units cube.

- Refer to the number 1,375 on the poster and explain how it is broken apart. Write several three- and four-digit numbers on the board and discuss the value of each digit.

- Draw a ten rod on the board. Ask, *What number does this represent?* (ten)

- Draw another ten rod on the board. Ask, *Now what number does this represent?* (twenty)

- Draw a third ten rod on the board. Ask, *Now what number does this represent?* (thirty) Tell students that when we count ten bars, we are counting in tens, or skip counting.

- Ask a volunteer to skip count in tens from 10 to 100.

- Say, *We can also skip count in hundreds.* Have the class skip count in hundreds from 100 to 1,000.

4

Relative Sizes of Numbers: Developing Meaning

- Write the numbers 12 and 21 on the board.
- Ask, *Which 2 is worth more? Which number is greater?*
- Make sure students understand that the place determines the value of the digit (2 ones or 2 tens). Write the numbers 215 and 349 on the board. Ask students how they can figure out which number is greater.
- Tell students to start with the greatest place (hundreds) and look at the digit in that place for each number. The number with the greater digit in that place is the greater number. For example, look at the hundreds place in 215 and in 349. The 3 is greater than 2, so 349 is greater than 215.
- Ask students what happens when both numbers have the same digit in the greatest place, as in 328 and 372. Make sure students understand that they need to look in the next greatest place. That is, they need to compare the digits in the tens place: 7 > 2, so 372 > 328.

3 Kinesthetics

Place-Value Tap!

Designate three areas of the room as "ones," "tens," and "hundreds." Say, *Everyone will run in place while I choose students to send to the specific areas. Then I will tap one person who must say what number is shown by the groups I designated as hundreds, tens, and ones.* Do this about 4 or 5 times.

4 Studio Weekly Log

- Have each student work with a partner to complete page 2 of the **Studio Weekly Log**.
- Early Finishers: Provide appropriate **Activity Cards**.

5 Conversation

Have students check to see if each of their answers is reasonable. Then go over the answers together allowing students to share solution strategies and ask questions.

6 Math Game

Place Value Game

Play in groups of 3 or 4. Give each student a copy of **Place-Value Grids BLM 4**. Players take turns tossing a number decahedron. The number each player tosses must be entered into one of the 18 places on his/her grid. At the end of 15 throws, students add the totals (using a calculator, if available).

7 Weekly Project

- Check progress and answer students' questions.
- Tell students to use the suggestions from their classmates to create a final list of between 10 and 20 items for their Snack Store.
- Tell students that they can make up the prices or find out real prices from a store.
- Explain that their snack store menu should include the name of the store, as well as a list of the snacks, and the prices. Students may decorate their menu or sign if they wish.
- Tell students to write five math problems for the store that ask about the lunch snacks they selected. The problems should ask about ones, tens, and hundreds.

8 Activity Cards

Provide appropriate cards for students to chose and complete. Remind students to record the number of completed cards in his/her **Studio Weekly Log**.

Writing Equivalent Numbers

Knowledge and Skills

- Read and write numbers through 9,999.
- Recognize equivalent representations of a number.
- Write numbers in expanded notation.

Preparation for Day 3

- Make copies, one per student:
  Fact Fluency 3
  Number Expanders BLM 5
- Take the number decahedrons from the kit. (Math game)
- Provide safety scissors.
- **Activity Card 309** is appropriate for this lesson.
- Provide materials for weekly project.

NCTM Standards

Number and Operations Standard

Understand numbers, ways of representing numbers, relationships among numbers, and number systems

- understand the place-value structure of the base-ten number system and be able to represent and compare whole numbers and decimals;
- recognize equivalent representations for the same number and generate them by decomposing and composing numbers.

1 Fact Fluency

Hand out **Fact Fluency 3**. Remind students to color in the graph to show the number of correct answers and to set a goal for tomorrow.

2 Instruction

Expanded Notation: Developing Meaning

- Tell students that there are many ways to show or say a number.
- Write the number 562 on the board and review the place values: 5 hundreds, 6 tens, 2 ones.
- Next to 562, write $= 500 + 60 + 2$ and explain that this is called expanded notation.
- Name any three-digit number, and ask a volunteer to write that number in expanded notation.
- On the board, write $200 + 40 + 7 = ?$ Ask a volunteer to write the three-digit number.
- Write the number 803 on the board. Ask students how they would write this number in hundreds, tens, and ones. Make sure students understand how to expand numbers with a zero in the tens place.
- Hand out copies of **Number Expander BLM 5**. Tell students to cut out and fold their expanders along the dotted lines, and then write numbers in the spaces provided. Tell them to open their expanders and read their numbers. For example, if a student writes 3, 6, and 8 in his/her number expander, he/she would say "three hundred sixty-eight" after opening it.

Equivalent Representation: Developing Strategy

- Write the number 36 on the board, and ask a volunteer to expand the number. (30 + 6)
- Ask students if they can think of any other way to represent this number. You may need to provide some examples to direct students' thinking. (20 + 16, 10 + 26, 9 + 9 + 9 + 9, 10 + 10 + 10 + 3 + 3, etc)
- Have students represent these numbers in as many ways as they can:

45	72	64

Reading and Writing Numbers: Developing Meaning

- On the board, write "three hundred twenty-five." Read the number aloud. Ask a volunteer to write the number.
- Write 726, 414, and 102 on the board. Have volunteers read the numbers aloud. Remind students to read 100 as "one hundred." Ask a volunteer to write each number in words. Make sure students are using hyphens properly.

3 Kinesthetics

Expanded Notation Sprint

Designate three areas of the room as "ones," "tens," and "hundreds." Say, *I am going to say a three-digit number. Then I will select students to hop to the hundreds, tens, and ones areas of the room in order to show that number in expanded notation. If you choose to go to an area where there are already enough students, you will need to go to a different area. For example, if I say 452, four students will go to the hundreds area, five students will go to the tens area, and 2 students will go to the ones area.* Do this about 4 or 5 times. Try to choose numbers whose digits add to the number of students in the class; for example, 452 works if you have eleven students.

4 Studio Weekly Log

- Have each student work with a partner to complete page 3 of the **Studio Weekly Log**.
- Early Finishers: Provide **Activity Cards**.

5 Conversation

Have students check to see if each of their answers is reasonable. Then go over the answers together allowing students to share solution strategies and ask questions.

6 Math Game

Writing Numbers Game

Play in groups of 3 or 4. Give each group a number decahedron. Players take turns tossing the number decahedron three times and recording the numbers generated. Each student then writes as many one, two, or three digit numbers as they can think of that are comprised of the digits on the decahedron. Each correctly written number is a point. Each student should have several turns throwing the decahedron. For example if the decahedron lands on 7, 4, and 2, students should write 7, 4, 2, 74, 47, 742, 724, 472, 427, 274, and 247.

7 Weekly Project

Check progress and answer students' questions.

8 Activity Cards

Provide appropriate cards for students to chose and complete. Remind students to record the number of completed cards in his/her **Studio Weekly Log**.

Predicting and Estimating

Knowledge and Skills

- Read and write numbers through 9,999.
- Learn a mental math strategy for addition.

Preparation for Day 4

- Make copies of **Fact Fluency 4,** one per student.
- Provide materials for weekly project.
- Take the number decahedrons from the kit. (Math Game)

NCTM Standards

Number and Operations Standard

Understand numbers, ways of representing numbers, relationships among numbers, and number systems

- understand the place-value structure of the base-ten number system and be able to represent and compare whole numbers and decimals;
- recognize equivalent representations for the same number and generate them by decomposing and composing numbers.

Compute fluently and make reasonable estimates

- develop and use strategies to estimate the results of whole-number computations and to judge the reasonableness of such results.

1 Fact Fluency

Hand out **Fact Fluency 4**. Remind students to color in the graph to show the number of correct answers and to set a goal for tomorrow.

2 Instruction

Making Predictions: Developing Strategies

- Tell students that when they add, they can use what they know about the numbers they are adding to predict what the answer will be.
- On the board, write $6 + 7$. Ask students if the answer will be more or less than 10. Ask volunteers to explain their predictions. (Both numbers are greater than 5, so their sum will be more than 10.)
- Have students predict whether the answer will be more or less than 10:

    $3 + 5$ $9 + 4$

- On the board, write $8 + 7$. Ask students if the answer will be more or less than 20. Ask volunteers to explain their predictions. (Both numbers are less than ten, so their sum will be less than 20.)
- Have students predict whether the answer will be more or less than 20:

    $12 + 12$ $8 + 14$ $11 + 14$ $8 + 8$

- Say, *A picture album holds 100 photographs. You have 51 pictures of your pet and 55 pictures that you took at the zoo. Do you have enough room in the album for all of the photos?*
- Ask a volunteer to answer the problem and explain his/her reasoning. (Both numbers are greater than 50, so the sum will be more than 100. There is not enough room for all of the photographs.)

- Say, *What if you have 49 pictures of your pet and 46 pictures that you took at the zoo. Do you have enough room in the album for all of the photos?*

- Ask a volunteer to answer the problem and explain his/her reasoning. (Both numbers are less than 50, so the sum will be less than 100. There is enough room for all of the photographs.)

- Repeat with number combinations of 81 + 14, 53 + 29, and 61 + 25

Estimating: Developing Strategies

- Say, *We can estimate the answer to an addition problem by looking at the numbers we are adding.*

- On the board, write 22 + 18. Below it, write the numbers 64, 31, and 40.

- Have students look at each number and think about whether it could reasonably be the answer.

- Ask, *Why can't 64 be the answer?* (Both numbers are less than 30, so their sum must be less than 60.)

- Ask, *Why can't 31 be the answer?* (22 is more than 20 and 18 is more than 10, so their sum must be greater than 30.)

- Ask, *Why can 40 be a reasonable answer?* (22 is a little more than 20 and 18 is a little less than 20, so their sum can be 40.)

- Have students estimate the answers and then explain their thinking:
    17 + 13   27 + 22   11 + 12

3 Kinesthetics 👥

Making Tens

Say, *I am going divide you into two groups, one large and one small. Everyone will run in place while the smaller group breaks apart and I point to some students who will move to the larger group to make a group of ten. Then I will ask one person in the smaller group to say a number sentence that tells how many students there are altogether. For example, if there are 8 students in the larger group and 7 students in the smaller group, two students will move from the smaller group to the larger group to make a group of ten. The person I point to will say "8 + 7 is the same as 10 + 5 = 15."* Do this several times, changing the number of students each time.

4 Studio Weekly Log 👥

- Have each student work with a partner to complete page 4 of the **Studio Weekly Log**.

- Early Finishers: Provide **Activity Cards**.

5 Conversation 👥

Have students check to see if each of their answers is reasonable.

6 Math Game 👥

Prediction Game

Play in groups of three or four. Students take turns tossing two number decahedrons. Each makes a two-digit number using the numbers in either order. For example, if a 2 and 6 are tossed, he/she can make 26 or 62. Each student tosses again and makes another two-digit number. Both will predict whether the sum of their two-digit numbers will be more or less than 100. Then each player must decide whether he/she wants to toss again to make another two-digit number. The goal is to get as close to 100 without going over.

7 Weekly Project 👥

Have students continue to work on Project 1. In addition to creating the chart, you might suggest that students make up problems like this:

- Max has 80¢. He wants to buy an apple for 45¢ and a pear for 30¢. Does he have enough money?

8 Activity Cards 👤

Provide appropriate cards for students to chose and complete. Remind students to record the number of completed cards in his/her **Studio Weekly Log**.

Rounding

Knowledge and Skills

- Read and write numbers through 9,999.
- Understand how to round two-digit numbers to the nearest ten and three-digit numbers to the nearest hundred.

Preparation for Day 5

- Make copies, one per student:
  Fact Fluency 5
  Number Lines BLM 6
  Weekly **Assessment**
- Provide materials for weekly project.

NCTM Standards

Number and Operations Standard

Understand numbers, ways of representing numbers, relationships among numbers, and number systems

- understand the place-value structure of the base-ten number system and be able to represent and compare whole numbers and decimals;
- recognize equivalent representations for the same number and generate them by decomposing and composing numbers.

1 Fact Fluency

Hand out **Fact Fluency 5**. Remind students to color in the graph to show the number of correct answers.

2 Instruction

Rounding: Developing Strategies

- Hand out copies of **Number Lines BLM 6,** one copy per student.
- Have students look at the number 18 on the number line. Ask, *Is 18 closer to 10 or to 20?*
- Have students look at the number 13. Ask, *Is 13 closer to 10 or to 20?*
- Have students look at the section of the number line between 10 and 20. Ask students which numbers are closer to 10 and which are closer to 20. Elicit that 11, 12, 13, and 14 are closer to 10; 16, 17, 18, and 19 are closer to 20. Explain that 15 is halfway between.
- Say, *It is easier to work with tens and hundreds, so we sometimes use the "nearest" ten instead of the actual numbers. This is called rounding. Rounding helps us check the reasonableness of answers, or make estimates.*
- Write several two-digit numbers on the board and ask volunteers to round to the nearest ten. Make sure you give a mix of numbers that are closer to the higher ten and closer to the lower ten. Provide at least one number that ends in 5 and further discuss what happens when a number is "between". (We round to the higher ten.)
- Explain that we can also round hundreds. Tell students to look at one of the blank number lines. Have them write 100 at one end and 200 at the other end, and put in marks at every ten along the line.

10

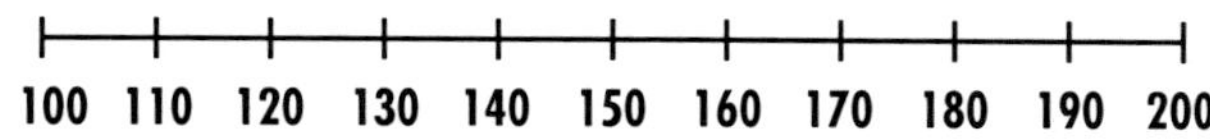

- Ask students where they would put the mark for 170. Then ask whether 170 is closer to 100 or 200. Elicit that since 170 is closer to 200 than to 100, we round up to 200.

3 Kinesthetics

Round!

- Have students stand around in the center of the room and do a few warm-up stretches.

- Say, *The left side of the room will be "10". The right side of the room will be "20". I am going to say a number and you have to decide whether it is closer to 10 or to 20. Then you have to go to that side of the room.* Repeat several times, changing the "closer to" numbers using larger numbers such as 70 and 80, 200 and 300, etc.

4 Studio Weekly Log

- Have each student work with a partner to complete page 5 of the **Studio Weekly Log**.

- Early Finishers: Provide appropriate **Activity Cards**.

5 Conversation

Have students check to see if each of their answers is reasonable. Then go over the answers together allowing students to share solution strategies and ask questions.

6 Assessment

Have students complete.

7 Weekly Project

Have students complete and present their projects. Have students share their charts and possibly read one of their word problems for their classmates to solve.

8 Family Letter

Have students complete the back cover of their **Studio Weekly Log**.

Your kit includes enough cards so that each student can have one Reward Card per week. Simply punch out the desired number of cards that match the riddle that is on the cover of the **Studio Weekly Log** for that week and distribute them to your students.

Addition Strategies

Knowledge and Skills

- Understand meaning of addition and subtraction.
- Add and subtract whole numbers through 9,999.
- Develop fluency with basic addition facts.

Preparation for Day 1

- Make copies, one per student:
  Fact Fluency 6
  Number Lines BLM 6 (Week 1)
  Operation Wheels BLM 7
  Project 2: *Animal Giants* **BLM 8**
- **Activity Cards 323, 324,** and **328** are appropriate for this lesson. Cards from the previous week may be used at any time.
- Organize materials for **Project 2, Animal Giants:** markers, paper, poster paper.

NCTM Standards

Number and Operations Standard

Understand meanings of operations and how they relate to one another

- understand various meanings of addition and subtraction of whole numbers and the relationship between the two operations.

Compute fluently and make reasonable estimates

- develop fluency in adding, subtracting, multiplying, and dividing whole numbers;
- develop and use strategies to estimate the results of whole-number computations and to judge the reasonableness of such results.

Summer Studio Reading Theme Connections

Animal Giants

1 Fact Fluency

Before beginning this activity each day tell students to first look at each exercise and try to answer it mentally. Hand out **Fact Fluency 6** and give students about 1 minute to work. Go over the answers with students and ask, *What strategies did you use?* Remind students to color in the graph to show the number of correct answers and to set a goal for tomorrow.

2 Instruction

Essential Question: *What are the meanings of addition and subtraction?*

Mental Math: Developing Strategies

- Brainstorm to elicit strategies that students use to add mentally.
- Draw a number line showing 0–20 on the board. Hand out copies of **Number Lines BLM 6**. On the board, write *6 + 5*.
- Tell students that when we count on, we find the larger number on the number line, and then count on the other number to find the total. Say, *Find 6 on your number line. Then, count on 5 more to find the total: 7, 8, 9, 10, 11.* So *6 + 5 = 11.* As you count on, draw the jumps along the number line on the board.
- Have students discuss how they might count on without a number line. (Use their fingers or make tally marks to keep track of the counting on.)
- Tell students that they can also use counting on for adding larger numbers. Draw a number line from 0 to 100 showing tens. On the board, write *30 + 40*. Have students put a finger on 30, then count on four more tens: 40, 50, 60, 70. So *30 + 40 = 70.*
- Have students find these answers by drawing number lines, if needed, and then counting on:
  70 + 90   110 + 40   1,600 + 300   120 + 70

Doubles and Near Doubles: Developing Strategies

- Say, *Sometimes the two parts that we are adding are the same. For example, 4 + 4 or 6 + 6. We call exercises like these "doubles."*
- Write the doubles facts from 1 + 1 to 10 + 10 on the board. Have volunteers tell the answer to each doubles fact.
- Ask students how knowing that 3 + 3 is 6 could help them add 3 + 4. If no one suggests it, tell students that they could use a *near doubles* strategy. Make sure that students understand that the sum of 3 and 4 is one more than 3 + 3. Write 3 + 4 = 3 + 3 + 1 on the board.
- Have students add the following examples mentally using the near doubles strategy.
  5 + 6   7 + 6   8 + 9   4 + 5   8 + 7
- Have students suggest how they could use the near doubles strategy to add 7 + 9 and 6 + 8.

Decomposing: Developing Strategy

- On the board, write 35 + 21.
- Say, *Numbers can be broken apart in different ways. For example, 4 can be broken into 3 and 1, or 2 and 2.* Ask students to break apart 35 and 21 in as many ways as they can. Ask which of the ways would be easiest to use to add the parts. Help students understand that breaking 35 into 30 + 5 and 21 into 20 + 1 would make adding easier. Ask, *What is 30 + 20? What is 5 + 1? Then what is 35 + 21?* (56)
- This strategy is called *decomposing*. Decomposing means "breaking apart."
- Write the following examples on the board. Ask volunteers to use decomposing to add the numbers mentally.
  43 + 26   24 + 32   18 + 61   55 + 33   74 + 14

3 Kinesthetics

Doubles!

Say, *I am going to call out a number and an action. Everyone will do double that number of actions. For example, if I say 2 jumping jacks you will double 2 and do 4 jumping jacks. If I say 3 toe touches you will double 3 and do 6 toe touches.* Do this 8–10 times.

4 Studio Weekly Log

- Have each student work with a partner to complete page 1 of the **Studio Weekly Log**.
- Early Finishers: Provide appropriate **Activity Cards**.

5 Conversation

Have students check to see if each of their answers is reasonable. Then go over the answers together allowing students to share solution strategies and ask questions.

6 Math Game

Addition Wheels

Play in pairs. Give each student a copy of **Operation Wheels BLM 7** and have him/her make up numbers to fill in one of the addition wheels with two-, three-, and four-digit numbers. Students swap wheels and solve as many exercises as possible in 2 minutes. Each correct answer is a point. Repeat with other addition wheels.

7 Weekly Project

Hand out a copy of **Project 2: Animal Giants, BLM 8** to each student. Have students work in pairs throughout the week to complete the project. If possible, have students perform additional research related to the project.

8 Activity Cards

Provide appropriate cards for students to choose and complete. Have a few counters, dot cubes, and number decahedrons set aside for card activity. Remind students to record the number of completed cards in the inside front cover of his/her **Studio Weekly Log**.

Subtraction Situations

Knowledge and Skills

- Develop meaning of subtraction.
- Add and subtract numbers through 9,999.
- Know a variety of subtraction strategies—both paper and pencil and mental.

Preparation for Day 2

- Make copies, one per student:
  Fact Fluency 7
  Part-Part-Whole BLM 9
- Display the **Subtraction** poster.
- Take the dot cubes from the kit. (Math Game)
- Provide materials for weekly project.

NCTM Standards

Number and Operations Standard

Understand meanings of operations and how they relate to one another

- understand various meanings of addition and subtraction of whole numbers and the relationship between the two operations.

Compute fluently and make reasonable estimates

- develop fluency in adding, subtracting, multiplying, and dividing whole numbers;
- develop and use strategies to estimate the results of whole-number computations and to judge the reasonableness of such results.

1 Fact Fluency

Hand out **Fact Fluency 7**. Remind students to color in the graph to show the number of correct answers and to set a goal for tomorrow.

2 Instruction

Subtraction: Developing Meaning

- Brainstorm to elicit what students know and understand about subtraction.
- Ask, *Can you think of some times when you or someone you know used subtraction?* (Figuring out change from a purchase, determining how many apples are left, and so on.)
- Point out the three scenarios of subtraction on the **Subtraction** poster. Talk about each one and show examples.
  1. Take away (There are 7 birds and 1 flies away; how many are left?)
  2. Find the unknown amount. (I had 25 stickers and I gave some away. If I have 11 left, how many did I give away?)
  3. Compare; how much more (If Jane read 7 books and Pablo read 5 books, how many more did Jane read than Pablo?)
- Read the following story problem to the class: *Kylie bought 24 earthworms. She put 6 in her compost bin. How many does she have left for her worm farm?* Have a volunteer point to the type of problem this is on the poster. (take away)
- On the board, draw this figure:

Part	Part
Whole	

- Tell students that this is called a *part-part-whole* box. Help them see that they can fill in the numbers they know to help them find the numbers they do not know.

6	?
24	

- Read the following: *Kylie bought 24 earthworms. She put some in her compost bin and the rest in her worm farm. If she put 18 in her worm farm, how many did she put in her compost bin?* Have a volunteer point to the type of problem this is on the poster. (find the unknown amount)

- Ask a volunteer to draw a part-part-whole box to help find the number of worms Kylie put in her compost bin.

- Then read the following: *Andre brought mealworms to school for a class project. He put 11 in a glass and 17 in a large paper cup. How many more did he put in the paper cup than in the glass?*

- Say, *Look at the poster and tell what type of problem this is.* (It is like the book example.)

- On the board draw 17 mealworms in a row and 11 mealworms beneath them so that they align one-to-one with the first 11. Have children explain how to find how many more are in the cup. (Count the worms that are not aligned with mealworms below.)

- Explain that for compare story problems, you can subtract to find the difference.

- Have volunteers make up story problems and share them with the class. Hand out copies of **Part-Part-Whole BLM 9** for students to use to help them solve each others' story problems.

3 Kinesthetics

Tap!

Say, *I am going to divide you into two groups. Everyone will run in place while I tell you how many students are in each group. Then I will tap one person and that person must say how many more people are in the larger group than in the smaller group. For example, if I say there are 8 students in the larger group and 5 students in the smaller group, the person I tap would say there are 3 more students in the larger group than in the smaller one. Then I will make new groups and do it again.*

4 Studio Weekly Log

- Have each student work with a partner to complete page 2 of the **Studio Weekly Log**.

- Early Finishers: Provide appropriate **Activity Cards**.

5 Conversation

Have students check to see if each of their answers is reasonable. Then go over the answers together allowing students to share solution strategies and ask questions.

6 Math Game

Number of the Day

Play in groups of three. Give each group two dot cubes. Choose a number of the day and write it on the board. (It should be greater than 12 to avoid negative numbers.) Students take turns tossing the dot cubes and saying the total of the two numbers tossed. Then he/she subtracts the total shown on the dot cubes from the number of the day. The person with the lowest number in each round gets a point. The first student to score 10 points wins.

7 Weekly Project

Check progress and answer students' questions.

8 Activity Cards

Provide appropriate cards for students to choose and complete. Remind students to record the number of completed cards in his/her **Studio Weekly Log**.

Subtraction Strategies

Knowledge and Skills

- Develop meaning of subtraction.
- Add and subtract numbers through 9,999.
- Know a variety of subtraction strategies—both paper and pencil and mental.

Preparation for Day 4

- Make copies, one per student:
  Fact Fluency 8
  Number Lines BLM 6 (Week 1)
- **Activity Cards 315, 316, 320, and 321** are appropriate for this lesson.
- Take the number decahedrons from the kit. (Math Game)
- Provide materials for weekly project.

NCTM Standards

Number and Operations Standard

Understand meanings of operations and how they relate to one another

- understand various meanings of addition and subtraction of whole numbers and the relationship between the two operations.

Compute fluently and make reasonable estimates

- develop fluency in adding, subtracting, multiplying, and dividing whole numbers;
- develop and use strategies to estimate the results of whole-number computations and to judge the reasonableness of such results.

1 Fact Fluency

Hand out **Fact Fluency 8**. Remind students to color in the graph to show the number of correct answers and to set a goal for tomorrow.

2 Instruction

Mental Math Ladders: Developing Strategies

- Write these exercises on the board and ask volunteers to solve them:

  $15 - 8 \qquad 24 - 17 \qquad 13 - 4 \qquad 30 - 18$

- Say, *I have a strategy that will help you do these. It is called a ladder strategy.* For $15 - 8$, start at 8 and count the steps to 15. First climb to 10 (that is 2 steps up), and then climb 5 more to 15, for a total of 7.
- Ask students why it is easier to climb to 10 or a multiple of 10 before climbing the rest of the way. (Because once you climb to 10, it is easy to see how much farther you have to climb.)
- Follow the same procedure with each of the examples above. Then have students do these exercises mentally by climbing mental ladders.

  $35 - 29 \quad 18 - 6 \quad 23 - 18 \quad 24 - 19 \quad 25 - 9$

Subtraction Patterns: Developing Strategies

- Write these expressions on the board:

  $9 - 6 \quad 90 - 60 \quad 900 - 600 \quad 9,000 - 6,000$

- Ask students what these expressions have in common. (All require you to subtract 6 from 9.)
- Write the answers to each of the examples. Ask students what pattern they see in the answers.
- Tell students that using patterns like this will make solving some subtraction problems easier.

- Have students do these exercises mentally by finding patterns.

  $4 - 1$ $40 - 10$ $400 - 100$

Counting Back: Developing Strategies

- Display a number line and write 58 – 24 on the board.
- Hand out copies of **Number Lines BLM 6**.
- Have students demonstrate counting backwards by tens and then by ones to subtract. They should start at 58 and make jumps by tens: 58 to 48 to 38 to 28 (3 tens), and then by ones from 28 to 27, 26, 25, 24 (4 ones). It helps to draw the jumps—large ones for the tens and little ones for the ones to show that $58 - 24 = 34$.
- Have students do the following exercises using the Count Back strategy.

  $62 - 31$ $47 - 23$ $55 - 22$ $38 - 15$

3 Kinesthetics

Climb and Hop

- Have students stand in one area of the room and do a few warm-up stretches.
- Say, *I am going to call out a subtraction problem. You will count your footsteps as you climb to 10 and then hop until you get to the answer. As each of you get to your last hop, stop and I will call on someone to give the answer. For example, I'll say 17 - 6. You will start with 6 and "climb" to 10 by taking 4 giant steps and counting out loud as you move. Then "climb" the rest of the way by hopping 7 times to get to 17. ($17 - 6 = 4 + 7 = 11$) Then I will start you on the opposite side of the room and call out another subtraction example and you will repeat the same directions.*

4 Studio Weekly Log

- Have each student work with a partner to complete page 3 of the **Studio Weekly Log**.
- Early Finishers: Provide appropriate **Activity Cards**.

5 Conversation

Have students check to see if each of their answers is reasonable. Then go over the answers together allowing students to share solution strategies and ask questions.

6 Math Game

Down to Zero

Play in groups of two or three. Give each group a number decahedron. Each student will also need paper and a pencil. One student chooses a two-digit number as the starting number, and each student writes that number at the top of his/her page. Students take turns tossing the number decahedron and subtracting the number they tossed. The first person to reach zero is the winner. Repeat, with a different student choosing the starting number each time.

7 Weekly Project

Check progress and answer students' questions.

8 Activity Cards

Provide appropriate cards for students to choose and complete. Remind students to record the number of completed cards in his/her **Studio Weekly Log**.

Adding with Regrouping

Knowledge and Skills

- Add and subtract numbers to **9,999**.
- Understand how to regroup tens and hundreds for addition.

Preparation for Day 4

- Make copies of **Fact Fluency 9**, one per student.
- Make copies, two per student:
  Hundreds Square BLM 10
  Tens Rods BLM 11
  Unit Squares BLM 12
- Provide safety scissors, and zip-top baggies.
- Take the dot cubes from the kit. (Math Game)
- **Activity Cards 317, 318, 322, 326,** and **327** are appropriate for this lesson.
- Provide materials for weekly project.

NCTM Standards

Number and Operations Standard

Understand meanings of operations and how they relate to one another

- understand various meanings of addition and subtraction of whole numbers and the relationship between the two operations.

Compute fluently and make reasonable estimates

- develop fluency in adding, subtracting, multiplying, and dividing whole numbers;
- develop and use strategies to estimate the results of whole-number computations and to judge the reasonableness of such results.

1 Fact Fluency

Hand out **Fact Fluency 9**. Remind students to color in the graph to show the number of correct answers and to set a goal for tomorrow.

2 Instruction

Regrouping: Developing Strategies

For this activity, you may want everyone to sit around a large table or in a circle on the floor.

- Hand out copies of **Hundreds Square BLM 10**, **Tens Rods BLM 11**, and **Unit Squares BLM 12**, two per student. Have students cut out the shapes, or you may cut them out in advance.
- Write $25 + 33$ on the board. Have students add these numbers mentally using the decomposing strategy. $(20 + 30 + 5 + 3 = 58)$
- Then say, *These are called base-ten shapes. If the squares represent 1, what is the value of the rods?* (10).
- On a table in front of students, place 10 of the rods together to form a square, and ask, *What is the value of the square?* (100)
- Ask, *How can we show 25 using these shapes?* Have students show 25 as 2 tens and 5 ones. Then have students show 33 using the shapes and add those shapes together with the 2 tens and 5 ones. Ask students how many tens and how many ones they have. (5 tens and 8 ones) Ask, *Is that the answer we got when we added mentally?*
- On the board, write $46 + 25$. Say, *Use your base-ten shapes to add these two numbers together.* Have students do this in pairs on the floor if there is not enough working space.
- Give students time to perform the addition. Then ask a volunteer to explain what he/she did. Make sure that students understand that 11 ones are the same as 1 ten and 1 one. Ask if

Summer Studio Math

anyone exchanged the ten ones for a tens rod. Demonstrate this for the students.

- Follow the same procedure for adding 64 and 53. Have volunteers explain what they did.
- Write these exercises on the board:

75 + 39   247 + 68   134 + 188

- Have students work together (sharing their shapes if they need to) to complete the exercises.

NOTE: You will be using the base-ten shapes tomorrow, so you may want to have students put them in baggies to keep in a designated place.

3 Kinesthetics

Add Around the Room

Say, *Everyone will jog in place. I will say a starting number and an add-on number. Then we will go around the room adding the add-on number to the total. For example, if I say to start at 7 and add-on 6, the first person will say 7, the next person will add 6 and say 13, the next person will add 6 and say 19, and so on. We will see how far we can get in one minute.* Repeat several times, with different starting numbers and different add-on numbers.

4 Studio Weekly Log

- Have each student work with a partner to complete page 4 of the **Studio Weekly Log**.
- Early Finishers: Provide appropriate **Activity Cards**.

5 Conversation

Have students check to see if each of their answers is reasonable. Then go over the answers together allowing students to share solution strategies and ask questions.

6 Math Game

Composing Numbers

Play in groups of three or four. Students take turns tossing a dot cube three times to make a three-digit number with the first toss being *ones*, the second toss being *tens*, and the third toss being *hundreds*. Players then write down pairs of three-digit numbers that will add to the number that was tossed. For example, if the three tosses resulted in 3, 6, 4 the number would be 463. Students could suggest 200 + 263, 100 + 363, or 203 + 260 as pairs of 3-digit numbers whose sum is 463. Each correct pair is worth a point. Pairs that require regrouping are worth two points. If a calculator is available, students can check their answers with it. After five rounds, the person with the most points wins.

7 Weekly Project

Check progress and answer students' questions.

8 Activity Cards

Provide appropriate cards for students to choose and complete. Remind students to record the number of completed cards in his/her **Studio Weekly Log**.

Subtracting with Regrouping

Knowledge and Skills

- Add and subtract numbers to 9,999.
- Understand how to regroup tens and hundreds for addition.

Preparation for Day 5

- Make copies, one per student:
  Fact Fluency 10
  Assessment 2
- Make copies, two per student:
  NOTE: You can reuse base-ten shapes from Day 4 if they are available.
  Hundreds Square BLM 10 (Day 4)
  Tens Rods BLM 11 (Day 4)
  Unit Squares BLM 12 (Day 4)
- Obtain safety scissors.
- Provide materials for weekly project.

NCTM Standards

Number and Operations Standard

Understand meanings of operations and how they relate to one another

- understand various meanings of addition and subtraction of whole numbers and the relationship between the two operations.

Compute fluently and make reasonable estimates

- develop fluency in adding, subtracting, multiplying, and dividing whole numbers;
- develop and use strategies to estimate the results of whole-number computations and to judge the reasonableness of such results.

1 Fact Fluency

Hand out **Fact Fluency 10**. Remind students to color in the graph to show the number of correct answers.

2 Instruction

- Revisit the essential question posed on Day 1: **What are the meanings of addition and subtraction?** Have children share examples in their own words.

Regrouping: Developing Strategies

For this activity, you may want everyone to sit around a large table or in a circle on the floor.

- Hand out copies of **Hundreds Square BLM 10**, **Tens Rods BLM 11**, and **Unit Squares BLM 12**, two per student. Have students cut out the shapes. Or, distribute the base-ten shapes that students created on Day 4.

- On the board, write 28 − 5. Have students subtract these numbers mentally.

- Ask, *How can we show 28 using these shapes?* Have students show 28 as 2 tens and 8 ones. Then have students subtract 5. Ask students how many tens and how many ones they have. (2 tens and 3 ones) Ask, *Is that the answer we got when we subtracted mentally?* (yes).

- On the board, write 34 − 18. Say, *Use your base-ten shapes to subtract 18 from 34.* Have students do this in pairs on the floor if there is not enough working space.

- Give students time to complete this exercise. Then ask a volunteer to explain what he/she did. Make sure that students understand that they can "trade" 1 ten for 10 ones, giving 2 tens and 14 ones. Demonstrate this to make sure that each student understands.

- Follow the same procedure for finding $43 - 29$. Allow students enough time to complete the exercise and then have a volunteer show how he/she solved it using the base-ten shapes. Be sure to describe the exchange of 10 ones for 1 ten.
- Write these exercises on the board:

  $55 - 19$ $\qquad$ $216 - 28$ $\qquad$ $300 - 134$
- Have students work together (sharing their shapes if needed) to complete the exercises. After students have completed the first exercise, have a volunteer explain or demonstrate what he/she did to solve it.

3 Kinesthetics

Subtract Around the Room

- Have students stand around the perimeter of the room and do a few warm-up stretches.
- Say, *Everyone will jog in place. I will say a starting number and a take-away number. Then you will go around the room subtracting the take-away number from the total. For example, if I say to start at 75 and take away 3, the first person will say 75, the next person will subtract 3 and say 72, the next person will subtract 3 and say 69, and so on. We will see how far we can get in one minute.* Repeat several times, with different starting numbers and different take-away numbers.

4 Studio Weekly Log

- Have each student work with a partner to complete page 5 of the **Studio Weekly Log**.
- Early Finishers: Provide appropriate **Activity Cards**.

5 Conversation

Have students check to see if each of their answers is reasonable. Then go over the answers together allowing students to share solution strategies and ask questions.

6 Assessment

Have students complete.

7 Weekly Project

Have students complete and present their projects. Have students talk about their animal giants and read one of their word problems for their classmates to solve.

8 Family Letter

Have students complete the back cover of their **Studio Weekly Log**.

Your kit includes enough cards so that each student can have one Reward Card per week. Simply punch out the desired number of cards that match the riddle that is on the cover of the **Studio Weekly Log** for that week and distribute them to your students.

Understanding Multiplication

Knowledge and Skills

- Explore multiplication as repeated addition.
- Understand and learn basic multiplication facts.
- Write multiplication equations.

Preparation for Day 1

- Make copies, one per student:
  Fact Fluency 11
  Multiplication BLM 13
  Number Cards BLM 14 (cut apart cards)
  Project 3: Creepy, Crawly Math BLM 15
  Creepy, Crawly, Hoppy Facts BLM 16
- **Activity Cards 329, 332, 337,** and **340** are appropriate for this lesson. Cards from previous weeks may be used at any time.
- Take the counters from the kit. (Math Game)
- Organize materials for **Project 3, Creepy, Crawly Math:** paper, drawing materials, index cards, large folders or envelopes.

NCTM Standards

Number and Operations Standard

Understand meanings of operations and how they relate to one another

- understand various meanings of multiplication and division;
- understand the effects of multiplying and dividing whole numbers.

Compute fluently and make reasonable estimates

- develop fluency in adding, subtracting, multiplying, and dividing whole numbers.

Summer Studio Reading Theme Connection

Creep, Crawl, and Hop

1 Fact Fluency

Before beginning this activity each day tell students to first look at each exercise and try to answer it mentally. Hand out **Fact Fluency 11** and give students about 1 minute to work. Go over the answers with students and ask, What strategies did you use? Remind students to color in the graph to show the number of correct answers and to set a goal for tomorrow.

2 Instruction

Essential Question:
How is multiplication related to counting and adding?

- Ask five volunteers to come to the front of the room and place both their hands, palms in, on the board for classmates to see. Ask, *How could we figure out how many fingers in all?* Encourage students to suggest possible strategies, such as counting all the fingers or adding groups of 5 or 10.

- Now point from hand to hand, as the class orally counts together by fives to fifty.

- Tell students that this is called "skip counting" because we "skipped" all of the numbers that weren't 5s.

Multiplication: Developing Meaning

- Have students tell what they know about multiplication. They will probably include these words or expressions: *times, factors, product, equal groups,* or *repeated addition.*

- On the board, write *4 × 3 = 12.* Ask students to explain what it means. Have them give some examples such as 4 groups of 3 children are 12 children or 4 cups with 3 beans in each of them equal 12 beans.

- Write *8 × 3* on the board. Ask students how they could find the answer if they did not know it. Students may suggest adding 8 three times (8 + 8 + 8), adding 3 eight times (3 + 3 + 3 + 3 + 3 + 3 + 3 + 3), or other ways to find the answer. For example, if 4 × 3 is 12, then 8 × 3 is 12 + 12 or 24.

- Write the following examples on the board. Have students use whatever strategies they want to find each answer.

    5 × 4   6 × 6   7 × 6   9 × 4

- Discuss each example and have students explain the strategies they used. All reasonable strategies should be accepted. Ask, *Which of the four examples was the easiest to figure out? Which was the most difficult?* Have students explain their thinking.

- Hand out copies of **Multiplication BLM 13**. Have students complete the worksheet and then discuss it as a class, or work through some or all of the exercises together.

3 Kinesthetics

Equal Groups

- Have students stand at their seats and do a few warm-up stretches.

- Say, *I will say a number and do a body action one or more times. When you hear the number, repeat the actions that number of times. For example, if I say the number 3 and jump twice, you should jump twice three times.* After each round, ask students how many times they performed the action in total (*i.e.*, if they jumped twice three times, they jumped a total of 6 times.). Make sure everyone understands the game, and then continue for several rounds.

4 Studio Weekly Log

- Have each student work with a partner to complete page 1 of the **Studio Weekly Log**.

- Early Finishers: Provide appropriate **Activity Cards**.

5 Conversation

Have students check to see if each of their answers is reasonable. Then go over the answers together allowing students to share solution strategies and ask questions.

6 Math Game

Multiplication Face-Off

Play in pairs. Give each student a set of number cards 1–6 from **Number Cards BLM 14**. Each student mixes the number cards and makes a face-down deck. Players take turns turning over two cards and saying the product. You may want to provide counters so that students can create equal groups. The player whose factor cards have the greater product wins that round and keeps the factor cards. When the deck runs out, each player shuffles the cards and play continues. The one with more cards wins.

7 Weekly Project

Hand out a copy of **Project 3: Creepy, Crawly Math BLM 15** to each student. Students may first work in a small group to plan a strategy for completing the project. Then they can break into pairs or individuals to complete each part of the project. Provide basic drawing materials: paper, crayons, markers, index cards for questions, etc. Distribute copies of **Creepy, Crawly, Hoppy Facts BLM 16** for students to use to generate questions. Provide folders or large envelopes for students to store their drawings and questions for Friday's quiz show.

8 Activity Cards

Provide appropriate cards for students to choose and complete. Have a few counters, dot cubes, and number decahedrons set aside for card activity. Remind students to record the number of completed cards in the inside front cover of his/her **Studio Weekly Log**.

Modeling Multiplication

Knowledge and Skills

- Understand and learn basic multiplication facts.
- Write multiplication equations.
- Model, draw, describe, and represent multiplication.

Preparation for Day 2

- Make copies, one per student:
  Fact Fluency 12
  Arrays BLM 17
  Centimeter Grid BLM 18
  Model Multiplication BLM 19
- Take counters and number decahadrons from kit.
- **Activity Cards 333, 334, 336, 338,** and **339** are appropriate for this lesson.
- Provide materials for weekly project.

NCTM Standards

Number and Operations Standard

Understand meanings of operations and how they relate to one another

- understand various meanings of multiplication and division;
- understand the effects of multiplying and dividing whole numbers.

Compute fluently and make reasonable estimates

- develop fluency in adding, subtracting, multiplying, and dividing whole numbers.

1 Fact Fluency

Hand out **Fact Fluency 12**. Remind students to color in the graph to show the number of correct answers and to set a goal for tomorrow.

2 Instruction

Multiplication Arrays: Developing Meaning

- On the board, draw a rectangular array of dots for 2 × 4 (2 columns of 4 dots).

  Explain that this arrangement of dots is called an *array*. Ask, *How many dots are in this array?* Say, *There are 2 groups of 4, or 8.* Ask students to describe the array with a multiplication fact. (2 × 4) Then draw an array for 4 × 2 (4 columns of 2 dots) and ask how many dots there are. Ask students to describe this array with a different multiplication fact. (4 × 2)

- Discuss what makes an array a good model of multiplication. (An array is formed by an arrangement of same-sized rows and columns.)

- Distribute counters to pairs of students. On the board, write 3 × 3. Have students make an array of counters to model this fact. (*3 rows × 3 counters per row = 9 counters*) Review that each number to multiply is called a *factor* and the answer is the *product*.

- Repeat with the factors 5 and 2 (*5 rows × 2 counters per row = 10 counters*) Compare arrays in different orientations, *i.e.*, 2 × 5 and 5 × 2. Ask, *What makes these arrays equal?* Elicit that 5 × 2 and 2 × 5 both represent 10 counters.

- Hand out copies of **Arrays BLM 17, Centimeter Grid BLM 18,** and counters students can use to

Summer Studio Math

solve the problem at the bottom of **Arrays BLM 17**. Have students complete the worksheet and then discuss it as a class, or work through some or all of the exercises together.

- Hand out **Model Multiplication BLM 19** for students to complete and discuss.

3 Kinesthetics

Factor Shuffle

Have students line up and count off 1 to 9. If there are more than 9 students in the class, start over at 1. Tell them these numbers are factors. Say, *I'm going to say a product, such as 6. When I do, those of you who are factor pairs of 6 will find each other and skip to the front of the room.* In this case, students with the numbers 1 and 6 will pair up and skip to the front. So will students with 2 and 3.

4 Studio Weekly Log

- Have each student work with a partner to complete page 2 of the **Studio Weekly Log**.
- Early Finishers: Provide appropriate **Activity Cards**.

5 Conversation

Have students check to see if each of their answers is reasonable. Then go over the answers together allowing students to share solution strategies and ask questions.

6 Math Game

Rectangles

- Play in groups of three or four. Give each student a copy of **Centimeter Grid BLM 18** and a pencil. The object is to outline rectangles on the grid without overlapping any. Explain that any multiplication fact can be shown as a rectangle formed by rows and columns, because each row or column has an equal number of squares. For instance, a rectangle that is 3×4 has three equal columns of 4.

- To play, students take turns tossing a number decahedron twice. The numbers tossed represent the length and width of a rectangle to outline on the grid. For instance, rolls of 5 and 7 become a 5×7 rectangle. Players count the squares within the rectangle and write the multiplication fact on the grid. For instance, $5 \times 7 = 35$. Players may outline and label that rectangle anywhere on the grid.

- Play continues until a player has insufficient space to plot the next rectangle without overlapping another. The winner is the one who has the fewest "free" squares remaining on the grid. Play several times, discussing strategies as they evolve.

7 Weekly Project

Check progress and answer students' questions.

8 Activity Cards

Provide appropriate cards for students to choose and complete. Remind students to record the number of completed cards in his/her **Studio Weekly Log**.

Multiplying: Zeros and Ones

Knowledge and Skills

- Understand and learn basic multiplication facts.
- Model, draw, describe, and represent multiplication.

Preparation for Day 3

- Make copies, one per student:
  Fact Fluency 13
  Number Cards BLM 14 (cut apart number cards)
  Multiplication Facts BLM 20
- Make copies, two per student:
  Hundred Square BLM 10 (Week 2)
- Take the money from the kit.
- **Activity Cards 333, 334, 336, 338,** and **339** are appropriate for this lesson.
- Provide materials for weekly project.

NCTM Standards

Number and Operations Standard

Understand meanings of operations and how they relate to one another

- understand various meanings of multiplication and division;
- understand the effects of multiplying and dividing whole numbers.

Compute fluently and make reasonable estimates

- develop fluency in adding, subtracting, multiplying, and dividing whole numbers.

1 Fact Fluency

Hand out **Fact Fluency 13**. Remind students to color in the graph to show the number of correct answers and to set a goal for tomorrow.

2 Instruction

One as a Factor: Developing Meaning

- Review the meanings of *factor* and *product*.
- Have a volunteer show a hand with 5 pencils in it. Ask, *How many pencils?* Elicit that there is one group of five, or five pencils. Then have five volunteers show a hand with one pencil in it and ask, *How many pencils?* Elicit that there are five groups of one, or five pencils.
- Ask, *How can I show 5 × 1?* Help students visualize that multiplying the factors 5 and 1 means either 5 groups with one object in each, or 1 group with 5 objects in it. Either way, the product must be 5.
- Challenge students to tell multiplication stories with a factor of one. Here are two examples:
  — There are 4 crackers in a package. Aisha ate one package of crackers. How many crackers did she eat? (1 × 4 = 4)
  — Mrs. Gonzales packed one book in each box. She packed 3 boxes. How many books did she pack? (3 × 1 = 3)
- Ask students what would happen if the numbers in one of the stories were switched. For example, if Mrs. Gonzales were to pack 1 box with 3 books, how many books would she pack? Guide students to understand that it doesn't matter what in what order the numbers are multiplied—the answer is the same.
- Have students summarize a strategy to use when multiplying by one. (Any number times 1 equals that number.)

Zero as a Factor: Developing Meaning

- Ask, *How can I show 5 × 0?* Help students visualize that multiplying the factors 5 and 0 means either 5 groups with 0 objects in each, or 0 groups with 5 objects in each. Either way, the product must be 0. Demonstrate this by letting hands be the group and pencils the objects. Have five students show a hand with no pencil in it and ask, *How many pencils?* Then show 5 pencils and no hands and ask, *How many people have pencils?*

- Hold up a dime. Remind students that one dime is worth 10¢. Ask, *How much money would I have if I had 3 dimes?* (30¢) *How much money would I have if I had zero dimes?* (0¢)

- Challenge students to tell multiplication stories with a factor of zero. For example, *Mike babysat his cousin for 3 hours. He earned $0 an hour. How much did he earn in all?* (3 × 0 = 0)

- Have students summarize a strategy to use when multiplying by zero. (Any number times zero equals zero.)

- Hand out **Multiplication Facts BLM 20** for students to complete.

3 Kinesthetics

Simon Says

Say, *We are going to play Simon Says, but I will give commands that include a multiplication. For example, if I say, "Simon Says hop 2 × 3 times." you will hop 6 times. For 1 × 4, you will hop 4 times.* Be sure to include commands with zero as factors. For example, *Simon Says to twirl 5 × 0 times.* The correct response would be <u>not</u> to twirl at all, since 5 × 0 = 0.

4 Studio Weekly Log

- Have each student work with a partner to complete page 3 of the **Studio Weekly Log**.

- Early Finishers: Provide appropriate **Activity Cards**.

5 Conversation

Have students check to see if each of their answers is reasonable. Then go over the answers together allowing students to share solution strategies and ask questions.

6 Math Game

Race to Zero

Play in groups of two to four. Provide each group with one copy of **Number Cards BLM 14** and two copies of **Hundred Square BLM 10**. The object of the game is to be the first to reach zero by subtracting the product of two number cards drawn at random from the current total. Each player begins with 200 points because there are 200 squares on his/her two number grids. In turn, each player picks 2 number cards to be factors. The player finds the product of those factors and crosses off that number of squares from their hundreds grids. The cards are returned for future rounds. Play continues in turn, with each new product crossed off the hundreds grids. The winner is the first player to have no squares remaining.

7 Weekly Project

Check progress and answer students' questions.

8 Activity Cards

Provide appropriate cards for students to choose and complete. Remind students to record the number of completed cards in his/her **Studio Weekly Log**.

Multiplication Patterns

Knowledge and Skills

- Understand and learn basic multiplication facts.
- Model, draw, describe and represent multiplication.
- Identify multiples.
- Identify and describe patterns in multiplication tables.

Preparation for Day 4

- Make copies, one per student:
  Fact Fluency 14
  Times Tables BLM 21
- Display **Multiplication Strategies You Can Use** poster.
- Take out paper, pencil, or markers.
- **Activity Cards 330, 331, 335, 341,** and **342** are appropriate for this lesson.
- Provide materials for weekly project.

NCTM Standards

Number and Operations Standard

Understand meanings of operations and how they relate to one another

- understand various meanings of multiplication and division;
- understand the effects of multiplying and dividing whole numbers.

Compute fluently and make reasonable estimates

- develop fluency in adding, subtracting, multiplying, and dividing whole numbers.

1 Fact Fluency

Hand out **Fact Fluency 14**. Remind students to color in the graph to show the number of correct answers and to set a goal for tomorrow.

2 Instruction

Patterns with 5s and 10s: Developing Meaning

- Together, count by fives from 0 to 100. Ask, *What pattern do you notice in the numbers you say when you count by fives?* (All end in 0 or 5.) Have students count slowly by fives again, but this time, ask them to stand for numbers that end in 5, and sit for numbers that end in 0.

- Explain that the products for a given number are called the *multiples* of that number. Explain that the numbers they say when counting by five are all multiples of five.

- Say, *Let's recite the multiples of 10. It's the same as counting by ten.* Together, count *10, 20, 30, 40 … 100.* Ask, *What is true about all the multiples of 10?* (All end in 0.)

Patterns with 2s, 3s, and 4s

- Together, count by twos to 20. Say, *Think about your age. Stand if your age is a multiple of 2.* Ask standing students to say their ages. If nobody has an age that is a multiple of 2, ask, *Who will be a multiple of 2 on his or her next birthday?*

- Together, count by threes to 30. Say, *Stand if your age is a multiple of 3.* Repeat the confirmation.

- Say, *Stand if your age is a multiple of 1.* Point out that everyone should stand because every whole number is a multiple of 1.

- Ask students to say the first ten multiples of 2 as you list them on the board. Ask, *What is true about all the multiples of 2?* (They are even numbers.)

- Ask students to say the first ten multiples of 4 as you list them on the board. Ask, *What is true about all the multiples of 4?* (They are even numbers and they are double the multiples of two.)

- Refer to the **Multiplication Strategies You Can Use** poster. Ask, *What is the skip counting number?* (7) *How can you describe the numbers 7, 14, and so on?* (They are multiples of 7.) Point out that with 6 skips you land on the product of 6 × 7, 42.

3 Kinesthetics

Multiple Hop

- Label four areas of the classroom with the factors 3, 4, and 5. Say, *I will say a number that is a multiple of 3, 4, or 5. Once I say the number, you will hop to the appropriate area. For example, if I say 6, you will hop to the area labeled 3 because 6 is a multiple of 3.* For a variation, you could specify different types of movement, such as taking giant steps, walking in slow motion, tip-toeing, or skipping.

- Begin by saying numbers that are multiples of only one given number other than 1 such as 9 (multiple of 3) and 25 (multiple of 5). Extend by saying numbers that are multiples of more than one of the factors such as 15 (multiple of 3 and 5); 12 (multiple of 2, 3 and 4); and 20 (multiple of 4 and 5). In these cases, discuss why students can go to different parts of the room.

4 Studio Weekly Log

- Have each student work with a partner to complete page 4 of the **Studio Weekly Log**.
- Early Finishers: Provide appropriate **Activity Cards**.

5 Conversation

Have students check to see if each of their answers is reasonable. Then go over the answers together allowing students to share solution strategies and ask questions.

6 Math Game

Product Tic-Tac-Toe

- Play in groups of three or four. Distribute **Times Table BLM 21** and a number decahedron to each group. Each player needs a crayon, pencil, or marker of a different color. To play, students take turns tossing the number decahedron twice to generate two factors to multiply. The first player locates the correct square on the grid for the product, and records the product in his or her color. Each player does the same, always recording the product in his or her assigned color. Point out that most factors appear twice in the table. Each player should write a product in both places (unless it is a double, such as 5 × 5, which will appear only once).

- Play continues until someone enters a product that completes a horizontal, vertical, or diagonal row of three squares. That player wins. Play can continue to determine second, third, and fourth places.

7 Weekly Project

Check progress and answer students' questions. You might want to suggest having students test each question and answer with a partner to be sure it makes sense, in preparation for their presentation on Friday.

8 Activity Cards

Provide appropriate cards for students to choose and complete. Remind students to record the number of completed cards in his/her **Studio Weekly Log**.

More Multiplication Patterns

Knowledge and Skills

- Understand and learn basic multiplication facts.
- Model, draw, describe and represent multiplication.
- Identify multiples.
- Identify and describe patterns in multiplication tables.

Preparation for Day 5

- Make copies, one per student:
  Fact Fluency 15
  Product Patterns BLM 22
  Three-Week Cumulative Test
- Display **Multiplication Strategies You Can Use** poster.
- Gather crayons or markers. (Student Edition)
- **Activity Cards 330, 331, 335, 341, and 342** are appropriate for this lesson.
- Provide materials for weekly project.

NCTM Standards

Number and Operations Standard

Understand meanings of operations and how they relate to one another

- understand various meanings of multiplication and division;
- understand the effects of multiplying and dividing whole numbers.

Compute fluently and make reasonable estimates

- develop fluency in adding, subtracting, multiplying, and dividing whole numbers.

1 Fact Fluency

Hand out **Fact Fluency 15**. Remind students to color in the graph to show the number of correct answers.

2 Instruction

Multiples of 6: Developing Strategies

- On the board, write 6×7. Ask students how they might figure out this product if they don't know it. All strategies are acceptable, but guide students to understand that if they don't know a 6-times fact, they can add on to a 5-times fact—they can find 5×7 and then add one more 7. Make sure students understand why this method works.
- Have students use the add-on strategy to solve these exercises:

  6×4 6×8 6×9

Multiples of 8: Developing Strategies

- Review the multiples of 2 by skip-counting to 20. Then review the multiples of 4 by skip-counting to 40.
- On the board, write 8×3. Ask students how they might figure out this product if they don't know it. All strategies are acceptable, but guide students to understand that if they don't know an 8-times fact, they can double the 4-times fact—in other words, they can find 4×3 and then double the product. $4 \times 3 = 12$ and $12 \times 2 = 24$, so $8 \times 3 = 24$.
- Have students use the double-fours strategy to solve these exercises:

  8×4 8×6 8×9

Multiples of 9: Developing Strategies

- On the board, write *9 × 3*. Ask students how they might find this product if they don't know it. Say, *I have a strategy that can help you. It is called the 10 − 1 (ten minus one) strategy. Multiply by 10 and then subtract the number that you multiplied.* On the board, write:
  $9 \times 3 = 10 \times 3 - 3 = 30 - 3 = 27$
- Have students use the 10 − 1 strategy to solve these exercises: 9×4 9×6 9×7
- Have students look for a pattern in the nines products. This pattern will help them check their answers. Guide students to see that the digits in a nines product will always add to 9.

Multiplication Facts: Developing Meaning

- Use the **Multiplication Strategies You Can Use** poster to review the various strategies for multiplying by the numbers 0–10. Ask volunteers to tell you about their favorite strategies, explaining it in their own words and saying why it is their favorite.
- Point out to students that if they know their 2s, 3s, 4s, 5s, 6s, 8s, 9s, and 10s facts, they only have to learn 7×7 because they have strategies for all of the other facts.
- Hand out copies of **Product Patterns BLM 22** for students to complete and discuss.

3 Kinesthetics

Multiplication Walk

- Have students spread out around the room and do a few warm-up stretches.
- Say, *I will say a multiplication fact and you will walk that number of steps. For example, if I say 4 × 2, you will walk 8 steps, but only in straight lines. If you come to an obstacle or wall, you may make a right-angle turn and continue. Try not to go to the same spot where you started. You can use any of the strategies we have learned to help you figure out the product—double-fours, add-on, 10 − 1, and so on.* Repeat 10–12 times, using a variety of multiplication facts.

4 Studio Weekly Log

- Have each student work with a partner to complete page 5 of the **Studio Weekly Log**.
- Early Finishers: Provide appropriate **Activity Cards**.

5 Conversation

Have students check to see if each of their answers is reasonable. Then go over the answers together allowing students to share solution strategies and ask questions.

6 Assessment

Have students complete the **Three-Week Cumulative Test**.

7 Weekly Project

Have students take turns presenting their projects to other groups. Encourage participation and give-and-take.

8 Family Letter

Have students complete the back cover of their **Studio Weekly Log**.

Your kit includes enough cards so that each student can have one Reward Card per week. Simply punch out the desired number of cards that match the riddle that is on the cover of the **Studio Weekly Log** for that week and distribute them to your students.

Understanding Division

Knowledge and Skills

- Explore division as sharing and forming equal groups or fair shares.
- Understand and learn basic division facts.

Preparation for Day 1

- Make copies, one per student:
  Fact Fluency 16
  Divide in Threes BLM 23
  Project 4: Prices, Yesterday and Today, BLM 24
  Prices Then and Now BLM 25
  Operation Wheels BLM 7 (use with Activity Card 354)
- Make copies, **Hundred Grid BLM 30,** two per student (use with Activity Card 346)
- Make a number line using masking tape. (Kinesthetics)
- Take counters and dot cubes from kit.
- Gather coins or buttons for game markers. (Math Game)
- Display **Meaning of Division** poster.
- **Activity Cards 343, 345, 350** and **354** are appropriate for this lesson. Cards from previous Weeks may be used at any time.

NCTM Standards

Number and Operations Standard

Understand meanings of operations and how they relate to one another

- understand various meanings of division;
- understand the effects of dividing whole numbers.

Summer Studio Reading Theme Connection

Yesterday and Today

1 Fact Fluency

Before beginning this activity each day tell students to first look at each exercise and try to answer it mentally. Hand out **Fact Fluency 16** and give students about 1 minute to work. Go over the answers with students and ask, *What strategies did you use?* Remind students to color in the graph to show the number of correct answers and to set a goal for tomorrow.

2 Instruction

Essential Question:
What are the meanings of division?

- Have students brainstorm what they already know about division.
- Provide students with counters. Say, *Take 18 counters and find out how many groups of 3 you can make.* Have students show how they found the number of groups. Some children may separate the counters into groups of 3 and count the number of groups. If no one suggests it, model how to take 3 at a time from the large group and count as you remove them (take 3, say 1, take 3 more, say 2, … take 3 more, say 6)
- Draw students attention to the **Meaning of Division** poster. Relate the example above to the first example on the poster. Say, *One meaning of division is to find out how many equal-sized groups you can make from a set.*
- Have students use counters to find the number of equal-sized groups like these: groups of 3 in 21; groups of 4 in 32; groups of 6 in 36.
- Say, *Take 28 counters and make 7 groups. How many counters will there be in each group?* Give students time to make the groups. Then have students explain the methods they used to answer the question. Some students may "deal" the counters into 7 groups until there are none left and then count how many counters in each

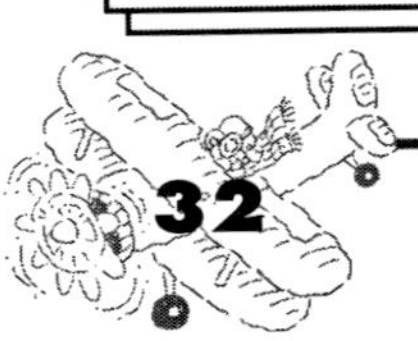

group. Others may take two at a time and place them in groups.

- Relate this to the second example on the poster. Say, *Another meaning of division is to find out how many in each group.*

- Have pairs of students use counters to divide the following examples: 22 into 2 groups; 35 into 5 groups; 39 into 3 groups.

Division: Developing Meaning

- Ask what students know about division. Discuss these words: *divide, divisor, quotient, equal groups, goes into,* or *fair shares.*

- Suggest to students that they can use skip-counting to divide. For example, to divide by 2, count by 2s until you get to the dividend and count the number of 2s it takes to get there. Model this by dividing the class into groups of 2 and count by 2s until everyone has been counted. Elicit the division fact. For example, if there are 12 students in the class, there will be six groups of 2. $12 \div 2 = 6$. Help students understand that the same number of students are counted each time, so the class is divided into *equal groups.*

3 Kinesthetics

Number Line Division

- Using masking tape or sheets of paper, make a floor number line from 0 to 30. Leave enough space between numbers so students can walk or hop along it. Bring students to the high end of the number line. Say, *We can use a number line to find out how many equal-sized groups..*

- Say, *How many groups of 5 in 30?* Model by beginning at 5 and "hopping" back toward 0, stepping on the numbers you would say when counting back by fives. Ask half the class to identify the numbers as you step on them: 25, 20, 15, 10, 5, 0, while the other half counts how many "hops" you need to reach 0. Then have one student at a time step out division on the number line as classmates call out stops and total number of jumps. Repeat with basic division facts, such as $30 \div 6$ and $27 \div 3$.

4 Studio Weekly Log

- Have each student work with a partner to complete page 1 of the **Studio Weekly Log**.

- Early Finishers: Provide **Activity Cards**.

5 Conversation

Have students check to see if each of their answers is reasonable.

6 Math Game

Divide in Threes

- Play in pairs. Each pair should be given a copy of **Divide in Threes BLM 23**, a dot cube, 2 game markers, and 50 counters. The object is to divide various numbers by 3 to collect counters.

- Place counters in a pile in the center. To play, one student tosses the dot cube, moves that number of spaces along the game board, and places a marker there. He/She also takes the number of counters and separates them into 3 equal groups. One of the 3 groups goes to the player, one is taken out of the game, and the third is put back in the center. The second student then takes a turn. Play continues until both players reach the FINISH star. The winner is the one who has the most counters.

7 Weekly Project

Hand out copies of **Project 4: Prices, Yesterday and Today, BLM 24** and **Prices Then and Now BLM 25**.

8 Activity Cards

Provide appropriate cards for students to choose and complete. Have a few counters, dot cubes, and number decahedrons set aside for card activity. Remind students to record the number of completed cards in the inside front cover of his/her **Studio Weekly Log**.

Relating Division and Multiplication

Knowledge and Skills

- Explore the inverse relationship between multiplication and division.
- Model, draw, describe, and represent division.
- Understand and learn basic division facts.

Preparation for Day 2

- Make copies, one per student:
  Fact Fluency 17
  Egg Carton Division BLM 26
- Display **Meaning of Division** poster.
- Take counters from the kit.
- **Activity Card 352** is appropriate for this lesson.
- Provide materials for weekly project.

NCTM Standards

Number and Operations Standard

Understand meanings of operations and how they relate to one another

- understand various meanings of division;
- understand the effects of dividing whole numbers;
- identify and use relationships between operations, such as division as the inverse of multiplication.

Compute fluently and make reasonable estimates

- develop fluency in adding, subtracting, multiplying, and dividing whole numbers.

1 Fact Fluency

Hand out **Fact Fluency 17**. Remind students to color in the graph to show the number of correct answers and to set a goal for tomorrow.

2 Instruction

Relating Division and Multiplication: Developing Meaning

- Ask, *What operation is the opposite of addition?* (subtraction) *What operation is the opposite of multiplication?* (division) Say, *Let's think about how this connection can help us divide.*

- Discuss the meaning of multiplication and division as opposite (or inverse) operations. Write $4 \times 7 = 28$ on the board. Review the meaning of each term. (4 groups with 7 in each group is 28 in all)

- Ask, *How could this multiplication fact relate to division?* Guide students to recognize that in a division situation, we know the total and how many groups, so we must figure out how many in each group. Or, we know the total number and how many go in a group, so we divide to find out how many groups can be made.

- Distribute 15 counters to each pair of students. Ask, *How many counters in all?* (15) *Suppose we were to make 3 equal groups. How many would be in each group?* Have students model this situation. Help them summarize their findings. (I started with 15 in all. I shared them into 3 equal groups, which gave 5 in each group.) Model how to write this: $15 \div 3 = 5$.

- Help students understand the relationship between multiplication and division. Say, *We divided 15 into 3 groups of 5, so we know that 3 groups of 5 make 15, or $3 \times 5 = 15$.* Ask volunteers to give the remaining related multiplication and division facts. Write all four

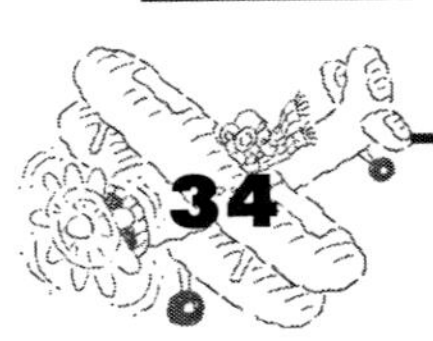

facts on the board:

$3 \times 5 = 15$, $5 \times 3 = 15$, $15 \div 3 = 5$, $15 \div 5 = 3$

- Draw students attention to the first two examples on the **Meaning of Division** poster. Write the four related facts for $30 \div) 6 = 5$. Repeat with $20 \div 4 = 5$.
- Continue by having students use the counters to model $9 \div 3$, $14 \div 2$, $10 \div 5$, and so on.

3 Kinesthetics

Division Relays

- Divide students into teams of four and have them do a few warm-up stretches.
- Say, *I will say a number. The first person on each team will fast walk to the board to write a multiplication or division fact for that number. That person will fast walk back to his or her team, and hand off the chalk to the next person. The next person will fast walk to the board and write a related fact, then return to his or her team and hand off the chalk to the next person. For example, if I say 45, the first person might write* $9 \times 5 = 45$. *The next person would have to write a related fact, such as* $45 \div 9 = 5$. *Continue until all four people have written a fact. The first team to write all four related facts gets a point.* Continue for 5 or 6 rounds using different numbers. Possible numbers to say include: 24, 28, 32, 35, 42, 45, 48, 54, 56, 63, and 72.

4 Studio Weekly Log

- Have each student work with a partner to complete page 2 of the **Studio Weekly Log**.
- Early Finishers: Provide appropriate **Activity Cards**.

5 Conversation

Have students check to see if each of their answers is reasonable. Then go over the answers together allowing students to share solution strategies and ask questions.

6 Math Game

Egg Carton Division

- Play in groups of three. Give each group a copy of **Egg Carton Division BLM 26,** a marker, and 36 counters. Have one of the students write randomly each of these numbers in two "eggs" on the game board: 1, 2, 3, 4, 6, 9.
- In turn, each student tosses a counter on the game board so that it lands on one of the numbers in the egg carton. Using the 36 counters, the student finds how many counters are in that number of equal groups. For example, if the counter lands on 4, the student must think, *How many counters will there be if 36 is divided into 4 groups?* (9) The student would earn 9 points. The winner is the first to get to 36 points.

7 Weekly Project

Check progress and answer students' questions. Be sure students understand what unit price means and how to find it by dividing.

8 Activity Cards

Provide appropriate cards for students to choose and complete. Remind students to record the number of completed cards in his/her **Studio Weekly Log**.

Finding Remainders

Knowledge and Skills

- Understand and learn basic division facts.
- Model, draw, describe, and represent division situations involving remainders.

Preparation for Day 3

- Make copies, one per student:
  Fact Fluency 18
  Shopping List BLM 27 (for project)
  Sharing Dogs BLM 28
- Take the dot cubes from the kit and obtain pencils and paper. (Math Game)
- **Activity Cards 344, 346, 347, 348, 349, 353, 355** and **356** are appropriate for this lesson.
- Display **Meaning of Division** poster.
- Provide materials for weekly project.

NCTM Standards

Number and Operations Standard

Understand meanings of operations and how they relate to one another

- understand various meanings of division;
- understand the effects of dividing whole numbers;
- identify and use relationships between operations, such as division as the inverse of multiplication.

Compute fluently and make reasonable estimates

- develop fluency in adding, subtracting, multiplying, and dividing whole numbers.

1 Fact Fluency

Hand out **Fact Fluency 18**. Remind students to color in the graph to show the number of correct answers and to set a goal for tomorrow.

2 Instruction

Remainders: Developing Meaning

- Invite two students to the front of the class. Hold 5 pencils. Say, *Suppose I want to divide these pencils equally between these students. What division problem would fit this situation?* Write $5 \div 2$ on the board. Ask volunteers to explain what will happen. Elicit that each students gets 2 pencils, but there will be 1 pencil left over. Point out that it wouldn't make equal groups to give one student the extra pencil, so we can call the leftover a *remainder*. Record the completed equation: $5 \div 2 = 2$ R1.

- Ask, *How would you explain this answer?* Discuss that it means that each of 2 people got 2 pencils, and R1 means "remainder 1," or 1 pencil left over that could not be fairly shared.

- Have six volunteers stand at the front of the room. Ask a seventh volunteer to distribute 15 sheets of paper equally among the six students. Ask a volunteer to describe this problem and write the division sentence on the board. ($15 \div 6 = 2$ R3) Repeat with other examples. Have students predict the answer before modeling the division.

- Go over the last example on the **Meaning of Division** poster. Make sure students understand that R3 is 3 remaining shirts.

- Hand out copies of **Sharing Dogs BLM 28** for students to complete and then discuss as a class, or work through some or all of the exercises as a group. Be sure students make the connection

between the last question and the concept of remainder.

3 Kinesthetics

Remainder Switcheroo

Have students stand around the room and do a few warm-up stretches. Designate areas of the room as 1, 2, 3, and 4. Say, *I will say a division problem, such as 18 divided by 5. You will divide and think of what the remainder is, and when I say GO, you will move to the area that matches your remainder.* If there is no remainder, stay where you are. Repeat as time permits, using divisors of 5 or less. After each problem, ask a volunteer to tell the division fact.

4 Studio Weekly Log

- Have each student work with a partner to complete page 3 of the **Studio Weekly Log**.
- Early Finishers: Provide appropriate **Activity Cards**.

5 Conversation

Have students check to see if each of their answers is reasonable. Then go over the answers together allowing students to share solution strategies and ask questions.

6 Math Game

Right Remainders

Play in groups of three or four. Each group needs a dot cube and a pencil and paper with which to keep score. The object of the game is to toss the dot cube, and then make up a division exercise that will have that number as its remainder. For example, upon tossing a 3, a student might say $19 \div 8 = 2$ R3. The other players confirm that the problem is correct. If so, that player earns as many points as the remainder. If the problem is wrong, the next person tries to make up a division problem with that remainder. That person earns the number of points in the remainder. Play continues in turn, with each person keeping track of his/her score. The first player to reach 21 points wins.

7 Weekly Project

Check progress and answer students' questions. Discuss items that students might want to put on a list of their own. Give each student a copy of **Shopping List BLM 27**. Have them ask older adults, such as parents, grandparents, or neighbors to compare present prices with prices from 50 years ago. You might want the students to ask their grandparents about DVD players, cell phones, roller blades, and other items that did not exist 50 years ago.

8 Activity Cards

Provide appropriate cards for students to choose and complete. Remind students to record the number of completed cards in his/her **Studio Weekly Log**.

Division Strategies

Knowledge and Skills

- Explore strategies to learn division facts.
- Learn basic division facts.

Preparation for Day 4

- Make copies of **Fact Fluency 19**, one per student.
- Make 8 copies of **Hundred Grid BLM 29**
- Take the dot cubes and counters from the kit.
- **Activity Cards 344** and **351** are appropriate for this lesson.
- Provide materials for weekly project.

NCTM Standards

Number and Operations Standard

Understand meanings of operations and how they relate to one another

- understand various meanings of division;
- understand the effects of dividing whole numbers;
- identify and use relationships between operations, such as division as the inverse of multiplication.

Compute fluently and make reasonable estimates

- develop fluency in adding, subtracting, multiplying, and dividing whole numbers.

1 Fact Fluency

Hand out **Fact Fluency 19**. Remind students to color in the graph to show the number of correct answers and to set a goal for tomorrow.

2 Instruction

Fact Families: Developing Strategies

- Review how division and multiplication are related. Say, *Let's explore some strategies we can use to figure out division facts.*
- On the board, write 42 ÷ 7. Say, *This means how many groups of 7 in 42 or 7 multiplied by some number equals 42.* Ask, *What multiplication fact could help us solve this division?* (6 × 7 = 42).
- Repeat with other division facts, such as 32 ÷ 8, 27 ÷ 9, and so on.

Dot Strategy: Developing Strategies

- On the board, draw 16 dots. Have a volunteer explain how you could use these dots to find 16 ÷ 4. (Draw loops around groups of 4, and then count the number of groups.)
- This is called the *Dot Strategy*. Tell students that they can do it on their own paper quickly. Repeat with various exercises, such as 27 ÷ 3, 36 ÷ 6, 21 ÷ 7, and so on.

Finding Halves: Developing Strategies

- Write the number 18 on the board. Ask, *What is half of 18?* (9) *How does this relate to a division fact?* (18 ÷ 2 = 9)
- Say, *When one student was asked to explain how she got the answer 5 when she divided 20 by 4, she said, "Half of 20 is 10 and half of 10 is 5, so the answer is 5." Is she correct? Do you think this will work for any number divided by 4?*

- Provide counters and have students try several examples to see if it works. After students have a chance to explore this, have them share their thinking. Draw 20 dots on the board. Say, *Let's see why this works. First divide 20 in half by circling groups of 10 dots—that's 2 groups. Then divide each new group in half again—that's 4 groups.*

- Have students draw dots and use the repeated halves strategy to demonstrate dividing 24, 28, and 32 by 4.

Dividing by 10s: Developing Strategies

- On the board, draw 30 dots and write $30 \div 10$. Have a volunteer circle groups of 10. Then write $30 \div 10 = 3$. Do the same for $40 \div 10$, $20 \div 10$, etc.

- Ask students to describe the pattern in the answers. Then ask them to use this pattern to do the following: $60 \div 10$ $100 \div 10$ $130 \div 10$

- Use 8 copies of Hundred Grid BLM 29 to help students learn how to divide by 100. Tape two hundred grids to the board and write $200 \div 100 = $ __. Ask a volunteer to circle groups of 100 and write the number of groups. Have students use the pattern to solve these: $500 \div 100$ $300 \div 100$ $800 \div 10$

3 Kinesthetics

Divide Around the Room

- Say, *I will say a starting number and call on a student. That student will say a division fact for that number and an action such as hop for the answer. For example, if I say 30, the first student might say 30 ÷ 6, and then hop five times. Then the rest of the class will repeat the fact and the action.*

- Continue around the room until each student gets a turn to tell a fact.

4 Studio Weekly Log

- Have each student work with a partner to complete page 4 of the **Studio Weekly Log**.

- Early Finishers: Provide **Activity Cards**.

5 Conversation

Have students check to see if each of their answers is reasonable.

6 Math Game

Zero Remainder

Play in groups of three or four. Have each student draw a 3×3 grid on paper and fill each cell with a different 2-digit number between 10 and 50 that can be divided by numbers other than 1. You might want to list the number choices on the board. In turn, each student tosses a dot cube. After each toss, the students cross out all of the numbers on their cards that have a 0 remainder when divided by the number shown on the dot cube. For example, if the dot cube lands on 4 and a student has 50, 16, 15, 27, 24, 8, 31, 42, and 18 on his/her grid, he/she could cross out 16, 24, and 8. The first player to cross off all nine numbers on his/her grid is the winner. However, the game is over when a 1 is tossed. Everyone then counts how many cells they have crossed out. The player with the highest number of crossed-out cells wins. Have students play several rounds. For each round, have students select different numbers for their grids. They should improve their choices of numbers as they realize that some numbers have more factors than others.

7 Weekly Project

Check progress and answer students' questions.

8 Activity Cards

Provide appropriate cards for students to choose and complete. Remind students to record the number of completed cards in his/her **Studio Weekly Log**.

Using Standard Division Notation

Knowledge and Skills

- Understand and apply basic division facts using standard division notation.

Preparation for Day 5

- Make copies, one per student:
  Fact Fluency 20
  Division Dots BLM 30
  Weekly Assessment

NCTM Standards

Number and Operations Standard

Understand meanings of operations and how they relate to one another

- understand various meanings of division;
- understand the effects of dividing whole numbers;
- identify and use relationships between operations, such as division as the inverse of multiplication.

Compute fluently and make reasonable estimates

- develop fluency in adding, subtracting, multiplying, and dividing whole numbers.

1 Fact Fluency

Hand out **Fact Fluency 20**. Remind students to color in the graph to show the number of correct answers.

2 Instruction

- Revisit the essential question posed on Day 1: **What are the meanings of division?** Invite students to respond in their own words.

- Ask, *When do we divide?* (to find how many equal groups can be made, to find out how many in some number of equal groups, to make fair shares)

- Ask, *What is a remainder?* (an amount left over after you form equal groups) *Why do some division problems have remainders?* (Not all quantities divide equally, so there are sometimes things left over.)

- Write $24 \div 6$ on the board. Then write $6\overline{)24}$. Say, *These are two ways to show division. The first way uses the symbol you have used many times. You read a division sentence like this from left to right, just as you read words.* Read it together as you track below it with your hand: "Twenty-four divided by six equals four."

- Say, *The other symbol also means division, but we read and use it differently.* Guide students to notice the position of the 24 in each case. Ask, *How are the two ways alike? How are they different?* Help students read the long-division by pointing to the 24 and reading it the same way as you read a number sentence. Also model how to read it as: *How many groups of 6 can you make with 24 things?*

- Show students how to record the quotient in both cases. In the number sentence, students write an equals sign ($=$) followed by the

Summer Studio Math

quotient. In the long-division method, the quotient goes above the line.

- In the example, erase the numeral 24 and replace it with twenty-four dots. Ask, *How can I use dots to show the answer to 24 ÷ 6?* Draw loops around groups of 6 and ask students to say how many groups. Write 4 above the line.

- Hand out copies of **Division Dots BLM 30** and have students use the division dots strategy to solve these exercises:

42 ÷ 7   48 ÷ 8   45 ÷ 5   21 ÷ 3   32 ÷ 4

3 Kinesthetics

- Have students stand around the room and do a few warm-up stretches.

- Say, *I will write a division problem on the board. I will say an action, such as jump or clap, and you will do that action the number of times in the answer. For example, if I write 30 ÷ 6 and say "jump," you would jump 5 times.*

- Repeat several times, varying the action. Use both styles of division notation: ÷ and)

4 Studio Weekly Log

- Have each student work with a partner to complete page 5 of the **Studio Weekly Log**.

- Early Finishers: Provide appropriate **Activity Cards**.

5 Conversation

Have students check to see if each of their answers is reasonable. Then go over the answers together allowing students to share solution strategies and ask questions.

- Choose a student to read the answers while the others mark their work.

- Encourage students to share solution strategies and ask questions.

- Have students make any needed corrections.

6 Assessment

Have students complete.

7 Weekly Project

Have students take turns presenting their projects to other groups. Ask volunteers to explain how they completed this project. Encourage participation and give-and-take. Invite questions and discussion. Be sure students understand how finding unit cost relates to the meaning of division—finding the number of objects in a group. Also talk about division meaning and finding "how many times more."

8 Family Letter

Have students complete the back cover of their **Studio Weekly Log**.

Your kit includes enough cards so that each student can have one Reward Card per week. Simply punch out the desired number of cards that match the riddle that is on the cover of the **Studio Weekly Log** for that week and distribute them to your students.

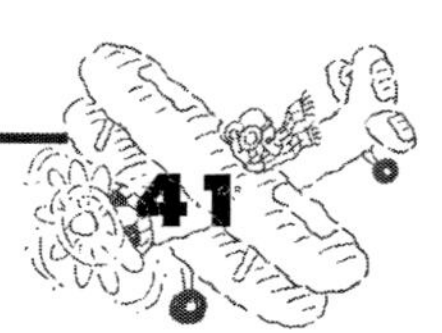

Developing Number Sense with Fractions

Knowledge and Skills

- Understand fractions as equal parts of a unit whole.
- Identify unit fractions ($\frac{1}{2}, \frac{1}{3}, \frac{1}{4}, \frac{1}{6}, \frac{1}{8}$).
- Identify halves and quarters of whole figures.

Preparation for Day 1

- Make copies, one per student:
  Fact Fluency 21
  Project 5: Mystery Math Day BLM 32
- Make copies, **Fractional Parts BLM 31**, 2 per student (Math Game and Project)
- Provide 3 × 5 cards, one per student.
- Take the dot cubes and coins from the kit.
- **Activity Cards 357, 358, 359,** and **360** are appropriate for this lesson.
- Organize materials for **Project 5: Mystery Math Day**: 4 x 6 index cards, 10 per student; small brown bag, or something similar, to use as a grab bag.

NCTM Standards

Number and Operations Standard

Understand numbers, ways of representing numbers, relationships among numbers, and number systems

- develop understanding of fractions as parts of unit wholes, as parts of a collection, as locations on number lines, and as divisions of whole numbers;
- use models, benchmarks, and equivalent forms to judge the size of fractions.

Summer Studio Reading Theme Connection

It's a Mystery

1 Fact Fluency

Before beginning this activity each day tell students to first look at each exercise and try to answer it mentally. Hand out **Fact Fluency 21** and give students about 1 minute to work. Go over the answers with students and ask, *What strategies did you use?* Remind students to color in the graph to show the number of correct answers and to set a goal for tomorrow.

2 Instruction

Essential Question:
What is the meaning of "fraction?"

- Draw a large square on the board. Say, *Suppose this is a sandwich to share.* Now draw a line (NOT through the middle) to cut the square into two unequal parts.
- Ask, *How many sandwiches do you see?* (1) *How many parts do you see in the sandwich?* (2) *Are they equal parts?* (no) *How should I redraw a line to divide the sandwich into two equal parts?* Ask a volunteer to explain what the two equal parts are called. (halves)
- Repeat the process by erasing the line and drawing lines to form three unequal parts, then thirds. Then repeat for four unequal parts and fourths.

Fractions: Developing Meaning

- Tell students that *fractions* are equal parts of a whole. Fractions are named for how many equal parts there are. Brainstorm with students to list some real-life uses of fractions, such as eating half a banana, watching a quarter of a football game, being eight-and-a-half years old, etc.
- List these words on the board: *half/halves, thirds, fourths/quarters, fifths, sixths, eighths,* and *tenths.* Help students read the words and link them to cardinal numbers (*i.e.,* thirds = three parts).

- Ask, *What kind of coin has a fraction name?* Show the coins when discussing them. (quarter; Some students may also mention a half-dollar.) Ask why this coin has this name. (4 quarters = 1 whole dollar).

- Review how to name a fraction. Draw a circle divided into sixths. Ask students to count the fractional parts and give their fractional name. Now shade one of the parts. Ask, *What fraction name is in the shaded part?* (one sixth) Continue with $\frac{2}{6}$, $\frac{3}{6}$, $\frac{4}{6}$, $\frac{5}{6}$, and $\frac{6}{6}$. Emphasize that the descriptive part of the fraction (sixths) is always included when you name the parts—one sixth, two sixths, and so on.

- Focus special attention on the notion of *halfness*. Distribute a 3 × 5 card to each student. Ask students to use a pencil to divide their card in half. Say, *Try to divide yours in half in a way that will be different from everyone else's.* Have students each show how they divided the card in half. As each student shows his/her card, ask, *How do we know that it is divided in half?* Students should understand that the two parts must be equal for it to be divided in half.

3 Kinesthetics

Fraction Action

- Say, *I will say a fraction word and an action. Your job is to do that action for the number of pieces there would be in an object cut into those fractional parts. For example, if I say* clap sixths, *you will clap six times. If I say* jump thirds, *you will jump three times.* Say words such as halves (2), quarters (4), fifths (5), and so on.

- Reverse the task. This time, say *I will clap my hands some number of times. Your job is to listen carefully, count silently, and then call out the fraction name for that number of parts.*

4 Studio Weekly Log

- Have each student work with a partner to complete page 1 of the **Studio Weekly Log**.
- Early Finishers: Provide **Activity Cards**.

5 Conversation

Have students check to see if each of their answers is reasonable. Then go over the answers together allowing students to share solution strategies and ask questions.

6 Math Game

Making Fractions

Play in groups of three or four. Each group will need pencils, two dot cubes, and a copy of **Fractional Parts BLM 31** for each student. In turn, students toss the dot cubes. The student who tossed the dot cube shades the figure on the **Fractional Parts BLM 31** that represents the fraction made by the two dot cubes. For example, if the dot cubes land on a 1 and a 3, the student would shade one part of the figure divided into three equal sections. If the student tosses a 2 and a 3 on the next turn, he/she would shade the 2 remaining parts of the figure divided into three equal sections. The player who first completely shades in one of the figures is the winner.

7 Weekly Project

Hand out a copy of **Project 5 Mystery Math Day BLM 32** and **Fractional Parts BLM 31** to each student. Have students use the shapes to make a matching game. Have them cut out and glue each shape onto a card.

8 Activity Cards

Provide appropriate cards for students to choose and complete. Have a few counters, dot cubes, and number decahedrons set aside for card activity. Remind students to record the number of completed cards in the inside front cover of his/her **Studio Weekly Log**.

Reading and Writing Fractions and Equivalent Fractions

Knowledge and Skills

- Model, draw, describe, read, and write fractions of a whole.
- Understand and identify equivalent fractions.

Preparation for Day 2

- Make copies, one per student:
  Fact Fluency 22
  Fraction Figures BLM 33
- Display the **Fractions** poster.
- Take the dot cubes from the kit. (Math Game)
- **Activity Cards 361, 362,** and **363** are appropriate for this lesson.
- Provide materials for weekly project.

NCTM Standards

Number and Operations Standard

Understand numbers, ways of representing numbers, relationships among numbers, and number systems

- develop understanding of fractions as parts of unit wholes, as parts of a collection, as locations on number lines, and as divisions of whole numbers;
- use models, benchmarks, and equivalent forms to judge the size of fractions.

1 Fact Fluency

Hand out **Fact Fluency 22**. Remind students to color in the graph to show the number of correct answers and to set a goal for tomorrow.

2 Instruction

Reading and Writing Fractions: Developing Meaning

- On the board, draw this figure:

- Ask, *How many equal parts are there in this figure?* (8) *What fraction names one part?* (one eighth)
- Write $\frac{1}{8}$ on the board. Help students identify and understand the parts of a written fraction: the bottom number (*denominator*) tells how many equal parts in the whole; the top number (*numerator*) tells how many parts to consider. Say, *One eighth describes one out of eight equal parts.*
- Draw circles or Xs in four of the boxes in the rectangle on the board. Ask, *What fraction tells how many boxes have Xs in them?* ($\frac{4}{8}$, or four out of eight) Have a volunteer write this fraction on the board. Repeat with other fractional parts of the figure. Refer to the **Fractions** poster. For this lesson, focus on the parts of the whole circle that are shaded.
- Hand out copies of **Fraction Figures BLM 33**. Have students draw fractional parts for each figure. Tell them to divide the figure so that its number of equal parts is equal to its number of sides. For example, the triangle, which has 3 sides, should be divided into thirds. You may want to show students how to use the dot to help them divide each figure.

Equivalent Fractions: Developing Meaning

- Refer to the rectangle on the board. Ask a volunteer to shade half the rectangle. Write $\frac{1}{2}$. Then ask, *How many eighths are shaded?* Ask, *Is $\frac{4}{8} = \frac{1}{2}$?*

- Say, $\frac{4}{8}$ *and* $\frac{1}{2}$ *are equivalent fractions because both name the same part of the whole.*

- Have students look at their completed **Fraction Figures BLM 33**. Ask, *Which figure is in sixths? How many sixths are equivalent to $\frac{1}{2}$? ($\frac{3}{6}$)* Repeat with similar examples for other figures. List equivalencies on the board.

- Ask students what pattern they see in fractions that are equivalent to $\frac{1}{2}$ (The numerator is half of the denominator.)

- Have students look at the figure in fifths. Ask a volunteer to tell whether or not $\frac{2}{5}$ is equivalent to a half and explain how he/she knows. (It is less than a half because the numerator is less than half of the denominator.) Repeat with similar questions.

- Ask a volunteer to explain how many thirds make a whole. Repeat with other examples. Guide students to understand in all fractions that are equivalent to one whole, the numerator is equal to the denominator.

3 Kinesthetics

Making Half

Say, *I am going to say a number. That number will be the denominator of a fraction. Then I will say an action. You will decide what numerator would make a fraction that is equivalent to one half, and do the action that number of times. For example, if I say 4, jump, you would jump 2 times, since $\frac{2}{4}$ is equivalent to $\frac{1}{2}$. If I say 10, clap, you would clap 5 times, since $\frac{5}{10}$ is equivalent to $\frac{1}{2}$. Repeat several times.*

4 Studio Weekly Log

- Have each student work with a partner to complete page 2 of the **Studio Weekly Log**.
- Early Finishers: Provide **Activity Cards**.

5 Conversation

Have students check to see if each of their answers is reasonable. Then go over the answers together allowing students to share solution strategies and ask questions.

6 Math Game

Tossing Fractions

Play in pairs. In turn, each student tosses a dot cube twice. He/She uses the numbers that came up to form a fraction whose numerator is less than or equal to its denominator. For example, with a toss of 4 and 2, a player can make the fraction $\frac{2}{4}$. If a player tosses the same number twice, such as 3 and 3, the fraction would be $\frac{3}{3}$. Players record each fraction they make. After 10 turns, players stop and look over their lists. They earn 4 points for any fraction that equals 1 whole, 2 points for any fraction equivalent to $\frac{1}{2}$, and 1 point for every other fraction. The player with the greater total score wins.

7 Weekly Project

Have the students shade the shapes so that each is a different fraction. On the other five cards, have them write clues that match each shape. Explain the rules of a matching game and allow the students to check each other's work by playing the game.

8 Activity Cards

Provide appropriate cards for students to choose and complete. Remind students to record the number of completed cards in his/her **Studio Weekly Log**.

Grouping Fractions

Knowledge and Skills

- Model, draw, describe, read, and write fractions of a group.
- Compute fractional amounts of groups.

Preparation for Day 3

- Make copies of **Fact Fluency 23**, one per student.
- Make copies of **Even Number Cards BLM 34**, one per pair. (Cut out cards or provide safety scissors for students.)
- Display the **Fractions** poster.
- Take the counters from the kit.
- **Activity Card 364** is appropriate for this lesson.
- Provide materials for weekly project.

NCTM Standards

Number and Operations Standard

Understand numbers, ways of representing numbers, relationships among numbers, and number systems

- develop understanding of fractions as parts of unit wholes, as parts of a collection, as locations on number lines, and as divisions of whole numbers;
- recognize and generate equivalent forms of commonly used fractions, decimals, and percents.

1 Fact Fluency

Hand out **Fact Fluency 23**. Remind students to color in the graph to show the number of correct answers and to set a goal for tomorrow.

2 Instruction

Fractions of a Group: Developing Meaning

- Brainstorm with students to find examples of real-world situations when they might need to find a fraction of a group, such as finding half of a class or sharing a bag of carrot sticks.

- Invite 10 students to the front of the class. Say, *Suppose I ask half of the students to face forward and half to face the wall. How many students would face each way?* (5) Record a fraction statement: $\frac{1}{2}$ of 10 = 5. Discuss how this idea links division and fractions. (To find half of a group, divide the number in the group by 2.)

- Say, *Suppose I asked $\frac{1}{5}$ of the students to put their hands on their heads. How many students would do this?* Write $\frac{1}{5}$ of 10 = ? Guide students to understand that to find a fifth, we divide the group into five equal parts. Ask a volunteer to tell how many students would be in each fifth. (2) Complete the number statement. Repeat with other groups of students and other fractions of groups. Begin with unit fractions, such as $\frac{1}{2}$, $\frac{1}{4}$, $\frac{1}{3}$, and $\frac{1}{5}$.

- Draw attention to the **Fractions** poster. In each case, count the number of circles and decide how many equal groups are called for by the demonstration. Have 12 students come to the front of the class. Ask how many students would be in $\frac{1}{4}$ of the group. Then how many are in $\frac{3}{4}$ of the group. Continue with $\frac{2}{3}$ and $\frac{5}{6}$.

- Distribute 15 counters to each student. Say, *You have 15 counters. You want to give $\frac{1}{3}$ of them away.*

How many counters is this? How many counters will you keep? Guide students to divide a group of 15 counters (the whole) into 3 equal groups of 5 counters each. Record the solution: $\frac{1}{3}$ of 15 = 5. Ask, *How much is $\frac{2}{3}$ of 15 counters?* (10) *How much is $\frac{3}{3}$ of 15 counters?* (15)

- Have students repeat the exercise, this time finding $\frac{1}{5}$, $\frac{2}{5}$, $\frac{3}{5}$, $\frac{4}{5}$, and $\frac{5}{5}$.

- Say, *We have divided our 15 counters into fifths and thirds. Are there any other fractions we can make? Can we make halves or fourths of 15?* (No, you cannot make groups of 2 or 4 out of 15 without having leftovers.) Guide students to understand that not all fractions are possible for a group.

3 Kinesthetics

Group Dynamics

- Form groups of various sizes that will be used to demonstrate a number of different fractions. Have each group stand in a different part of the room and do a few warm-up stretches.

- Say, *I will ask a fraction of each group to do an action. For example, I might ask $\frac{1}{2}$ of Group A to twirl around. After each direction, talk with your group. Figure out how many people should twirl and how many should stay still. Then we'll try other fractions and directions. I might ask $\frac{1}{4}$ of Group B to touch their toes. Be sure to take turns so that everyone gets to move, but you all agree on how many people move each time.*

- Make sure you use fractions that are appropriate to the size of each group. For example, if there are three students in a group, use thirds. If there are four students in a group, use halves or fourths. Repeat as time permits.

- Say, *I'd like $\frac{0}{15}$* (use the appropriate denominator for the class) *of you to whistle.* Pause as students decide what to do. *I'd like $\frac{15}{15}$* (or whatever fraction is all) *of the class to return to their seats.*

4 Studio Weekly Log

- Have each student work with a partner to complete page 3 of the **Studio Weekly Log**.

- Early Finishers: Provide appropriate **Activity Cards**.

5 Conversation

Have students check to see if each of their answers is reasonable. Then go over the answers together allowing students to share solution strategies and ask questions.

6 Math Game

Finding Half

Play in groups of three or four. Each group will need 60 counters, a copy of **Even Number Cards BLM 34**, and a pair of safety scissors. Students cut out the cards, shuffle them, and put them face down. In turn, a student turns a card up. That student takes the number of counters shown on the card and then finds half of the number. The student gets that number of points. For example, if the student turns over a 12, he/she gets 6 points since 6 is half of 12. Students take turns turning over the cards and taking counters. Repeat the game, finding one fourth instead of half. At the end of play, the students with the most points wins.

7 Weekly Project

Check progress and answer students' questions.

8 Activity Cards

Provide appropriate cards for students to choose and complete. Remind students to record the number of completed cards in his/her **Studio Weekly Log**.

Using Visual Models and Benchmarks

Knowledge and Skills

- Develop mental math strategies for comparing fractions to halves and wholes.
- Develop visual and spatial sense for working with fractional amounts.

Preparation for Day 4

- Make copies, one per student:
  Fact Fluency 24
  Fraction Strips BLM 35
  Estimating Fractions BLM 36
  Hundred Square BLM 10 (Week 2)
- **Activity Cards 366** and **368** are appropriate for this lesson.
- Take the dot cubes from the kit. (Math Game)
- Provide materials for weekly project.

NCTM Standards

Number and Operations Standard

Understand numbers, ways of representing numbers, relationships among numbers, and number systems

- use models, benchmarks, and equivalent forms to judge the size of fractions.

1 Fact Fluency

Hand out **Fact Fluency 24**. Remind students to color in the graph to show the number of correct answers and to set a goal for tomorrow.

2 Instruction

Using Visual Models and Benchmarks: Developing Strategies

- Draw a number line on the board and review the whole numbers with students. Draw a half mark between 0 and 1. Ask, *What fraction does this show?* Tell the students that between each whole number there are fractional parts.
- Hand out copies of **Fraction Strips BLM 35**. Have students cut out the strips and use them to make a set of fraction bars. Guide the students to line up the fraction strips along the 0 ends like number lines.
- Have students use their strips to compare fractions. Ask comparison questions such as these:

  Which is greater: $\frac{1}{4}$ or $\frac{1}{3}$?

  Which is closer to 1 whole: $\frac{2}{3}$ or $\frac{7}{8}$?

  Which is nearer to half: $\frac{1}{3}$ or $\frac{6}{8}$?

- Have students explain how to compare $\frac{2}{3}$ and $\frac{7}{8}$ using that same strategy. Guide students to line up the fraction strips along the 0 ends (like number lines) to prove their answers.

Adding and Subtracting Fractions: Developing Mental Math

- List some fractions that represent wholes, such as $\frac{5}{5}$, $\frac{6}{6}$, $\frac{8}{8}$, $\frac{10}{10}$, etc.
- On the board, write the fraction $\frac{9}{9}$. Say *Suppose I eat $\frac{5}{9}$ of a banana. What fractional part do I have to eat in order to eat the whole thing? How do you know?* ($\frac{4}{9}$, because $\frac{5}{9}$ and $\frac{4}{9}$ make $\frac{9}{9}$, which is

48

1 whole) Ask similar questions for students to answer using mental math.

- Tell students that another strategy is to think about half. Ask a volunteer to explain what is true about all fractions equivalent to one half. (The numerator is half of the denominator.) Say, *Mario built $\frac{5}{8}$ of a wall. Is this more or less than half? How do you know?* (more, because half would be $\frac{4}{8}$, and $\frac{5}{8}$ is one more eighth) Pose similar questions.

- Have students complete **Estimating Fractions BLM 36**.

3 Kinesthetics

Benchmark Dash

Designate one side of the room "More than Half" and the other side of the room "Less than Half". Say, *I am going to say a fraction. You have to decide whether it is more than half or less than half and move to that side of the room. For example, if I say $\frac{3}{5}$, you will move to the* "More than Half" *side of the room. If I say $\frac{1}{8}$, you will move to the* "Less than Half" *side of the room.* Repeat several times. Use a variety of fractions with denominators less than 10.

4 Studio Weekly Log

- Have each student work with a partner to complete page 4 of the **Studio Weekly Log**.

- Early Finishers: Provide appropriate **Activity Cards**.

5 Conversation

Have students check to see if each of their answers is reasonable. Then go over the answers together allowing students to share solution strategies and ask questions.

6 Math Game

Fraction Grids

Play in small groups. Each group needs two dot cubes and a copy of **Hundred Square BLM 10** for each student. In turn, each student tosses the dot cubes and makes a fraction that is less than or equal to 1 out of the numbers tossed. For example, if a student tosses a 2 and 4, he/she would make a fraction of $\frac{2}{4}$. If the student tosses the same number of both cubes, he/she tosses again. The student then colors in the number of empty squares on the hundred square that is equivalent to the fraction tossed. For example, if there are 100 empty squares and the student tosses a 2 and a 4, he/she would color in $\frac{2}{4}$ of 100 squares, or 50 squares. If the number of empty squares cannot be equally divided into the fraction thrown, that student loses his/her turn. For example, if the student has 9 empty squares and tosses a 1 and a 4, he/she has to wait until his/her next turn because 9 cannot be divided into quarters. The winner is the student who fills in his/her hundred square first, or the one who has the most squares filled in when time runs out.

7 Weekly Project

Give the students a few more examples of "Who Am I" puzzles, such as, those who have brown eyes, blond hair, play the piano, etc. Explain that for the clues to always be true, the descriptions must be something that doesn't change. Colors of clothes can change, but colors of eyes cannot.

8 Activity Cards

Provide appropriate cards for students to choose and complete. Remind students to record the number of completed cards in his/her **Studio Weekly Log**.

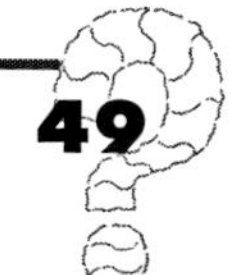

Measuring with Fractions

Knowledge and Skills

- Understand and apply fraction concepts to linear measurement (in fractions of inches).

Preparation for Day 5

- Make copies, one per student:
  Fact Fluency 25
  Inch Ruler BLM 37
  Weekly Assessment
- **Activity Cards 369** and **370** are appropriate for this lesson.
- Draw lines on the board as described in the Kinesthetics activity, and have two 12-inch rulers available.
- Provide safety scissors.
- Display the **Fractions** poster.
- Provide materials for weekly project.

NCTM Standards

Number and Operations Standard

Understand numbers, ways of representing numbers, relationships among numbers, and number systems

- develop understanding of fractions as parts of unit wholes, as parts of a collection, as locations on number lines, and as division of whole numbers
- use models, benchmarks and equivalent forms to judge the size of fractions
- recognize and generate equivalent forms of commonly used fractions

1 Fact Fluency

Hand out **Fact Fluency 25**. Remind students to color in the graph to show the number of correct answers.

2 Instruction

Fractional Measurements: Developing Meaning

- Revisit the essential question posed on Day 1: **What is the meaning of "fractions?"** Use the **Fractions** poster to review the meanings of fractions: parts of a whole and parts of a group. Ask, *When and where do we use fractions in our lives?* Invite students to respond in their own words with examples from their experience and this week's work.

- If measurement is not mentioned, explain that people often use fractions when they measure with an inch ruler. Most things are not exactly 1 inch, 2 inches, 3 inches, and so on, in length. Lengths often fall between whole inches.

- Explain that we can give lengths using fractions and whole numbers together. Distribute copies of **Inch Ruler BLM 37** and have students cut it out.

- Have students look at the ruler. Tell them to point to each whole number they see; explain that these numbers show inches.

- Ask, *How long is this ruler?* (10 inches) Ask a volunteer to explain what the little marks between whole numbers mean. (fractions of inches) Guide students to identify the marks that indicate $\frac{1}{2}$, $\frac{1}{4}$, and $\frac{3}{4}$ inches. Review that $\frac{2}{4}$ is equivalent to $\frac{1}{2}$.

- Say, *Think of the ruler as a number line. At the far left would be zero, though there is no zero on many rulers. Between each whole number are fractional parts just like a number line.*

- Point to the half mark between 1 and 2. Check that students are pointing accurately. Say, *We call this one and a half. It is more than 1, but less than 2.* On the board, show students how this is written: $1\frac{1}{2}$. Continue saying and writing various mixed number amounts on the board and ask students to locate each position on the ruler. As you work, encourage students to recall what they have been learning about fractions.

Measurement with Benchmarks: Developing Meaning

Gather small items from the classroom, such as paperclips, erasers, stickers, push pins, etc. Have students use their rulers to decide whether each item's length is closest to $\frac{1}{2}$ inch, 1 inch, $1\frac{1}{2}$ inches, or 2 inches.

3 Kinesthetics

Measurement Relay

- Mark off two large sections of the board and label one Section A and the other Section B. In Section A, randomly draw about 10 line segments ranging in length from 1 to 10 inches including several that are mixed numbers, such as $1\frac{1}{2}$, $3\frac{1}{4}$, and so on. Draw 10 lines of the exact same lengths in Section B of the board, but arrange them differently from those in Section A. Next in each section, make a list of the measurements of the line segments in order from least to greatest.

- Form two teams and identify each as A or B. Have students form lines and give the first person on each team a ruler. Say, *We are going to have a relay race. Each team needs to find a line segment that matches one of the measurements on the list. When I say "Go," the first person on each team takes a ruler, races to the board, measures a line, and puts a check by its length in his/her team's list. That student then races back to his/her team, gives the ruler to the second person who goes to the board, measures another line, and marks its measurement off the list.* Play continues until one team has measured lines and marked off all the measurements on the appropriate list.

4 Studio Weekly Log

- Have each student work with a partner to complete page 5 of the **Studio Weekly Log**.
- Early Finishers: Provide appropriate **Activity Cards**.

5 Conversation

Have students check to see if each of their answers is reasonable. Then go over the answers together allowing students to share solution strategies and ask questions.

6 Assessment

Have students complete.

7 Weekly Project

Place the students' "Who Am I" puzzles in the grab bag. Have the students pull them out one by one and solve the riddles.

8 Family Letter

Have students turn to the back cover of their **Studio Weekly Log**. Tell students to write a letter to their family about what they learned in math class this week.

Your kit includes enough cards so that each student can have one Reward Card per week. Simply punch out the desired number of cards that match the riddle that is on the cover of the **Studio Weekly Log** for that week and distribute them to your students.

Relating Decimals and Fractions

Knowledge and Skills

- Understand the relationship between fractions and decimals.
- Recognize common equivalent forms of fractions and decimals.

Preparation for Day 1

- Make copies, one per student:
  Fact Fluency 26
  Project 6: Decimal Party Plan BLM 38
  Memory Math Game BLM 39
- Take coins from the kit.
- Provide safety scissors, crayons and markers.
- Obtain index cards and prepare as directed in Kinesthetics. (Save for Day 3)
- **Activity Cards 377, 378,** and **379** are appropriate for this lesson.

NCTM Standards

Number and Operations Standard

Understand numbers, ways of representing numbers, relationships among numbers, and number systems

- understand the place-value structure of the base-ten number system and be able to represent and compare whole numbers and decimals;
- recognize and generate equivalent forms of commonly used fractions, decimals, and percents.

Summer Studio Reading Theme Connection

Be Our Guest!

1 Fact Fluency

Before beginning this activity each day tell students to first look at each exercise and try to answer it mentally. Hand out **Fact Fluency 26** and give students about 1 minute to work. Go over the answers with students and ask, *What strategies did you use?* Remind students to color in the graph to show the number of correct answers and to set a goal for tomorrow.

2 Instruction

Essential Question:
What is the meaning of a decimal point?

- Remind students that they have learned to use fractions to name parts of a whole. Say, *There is another way to write fractions to name parts of a whole.* Write the decimal *0.5* on the board. Ask students if they have ever seen a number written in this way. Say, *You can recognize this as a decimal because it has a dot called a decimal point.* Point to the decimal point. *Where do you often see decimal points?* (in money amounts, in sports statistics) Say, *This decimal number isn't written like a fraction, but it describes part of a whole.*

Equivalent Fractions and Decimals: Developing Meaning

- On the board, draw this figure:

- Shade in one section of the figure and ask a volunteer to tell what fraction is shaded. ($\frac{1}{10}$) Explain that this fraction can also be expressed as a decimal: 0.1. Fractions and decimals can both be used to show tenths.

- Tell students that other fractions can also be expressed as decimals. Distribute coins to pairs of students. Say, *Money amounts are often written as decimals. You can use your understanding of money to help you recognize equivalent decimals and fractions.*

- Ask, *What coin has the value of a quarter of a dollar?* (quarter) Have students show this coin. Ask a volunteer to tell the decimal that means the same as $\frac{1}{4}$? (0.25). Continue with 50¢, $\frac{1}{2}$, and 0.5, then with 75¢, $\frac{3}{4}$, and 0.75.

3 Kinesthetics

Decimal Match

- Use index cards to create a pack of cards that show matching statements in tenths and hundredths. For example, on one card write 0.7, on another write 7 out of 10, and on a third write $\frac{7}{10}$. Make cards that show tenths and fourths. Mix the cards and distribute one card to each student.

- Say, *I will give each student a card. On my signal, you must find the other two people whose cards mean the same thing as your card. For example, if your card says 0.1, you will need to find the people whose cards say $\frac{1}{10}$ and 1 out of 10. When you find your group, you will explain why your cards match.*

- Repeat as time permits.

4 Studio Weekly Log

- Have each student work with a partner to complete page 1 of the **Studio Weekly Log**.
- Early Finishers: Provide **Activity Cards**.

5 Conversation

Have students check to see if each of their answers is reasonable. Then go over the answers together allowing students to share solution strategies and ask questions.

6 Math Game

Memory

Play in pairs. Hand out **Memory Math Game BLM 39**. Allow students to cut out cards and then randomly place the cards face-down in an array. In turn, players turn over one card, look at it, and try to find the card with its fraction or decimal equivalent. If the player chooses the correct card, he or she keeps the pair. If the player chooses an incorrect card, he or she returns both cards to their original positions, face-down. Students must pay careful attention to the cards that other players turn over, so they can locate the cards they need. When all of the pairs have been found, the player with the most pairs of cards wins.

7 Weekly Project

Hand out a copy of **Project 6: Decimal Party Plan BLM 38** to each student. Tell students that the number of people coming to the party is all the class and you. That's the number to use when counting by 5s.

8 Activity Cards

Provide appropriate cards for students to choose and complete. Remind students to record the number of completed cards in the inside cover of his/her **Studio Weekly Log**.

Understanding Tenths and Hundredths

Knowledge and Skills

- Understand the concept of decimal numbers in tenths and hundredths.
- Model, describe, show, read, and write decimals in tenths and hundreds.

Preparation for Day 2

- Make copies, one per student:
  Fact Fluency 27
  Decimal Grids BLM 40 (8 copies)
  Hundred Square BLM 10 (Week 2)
- Take the number decahedrons from the kit. (Math Game)
- Make labels for room. (Kinesthetics)
- Gather crayons, safety scissors, tape, and markers.
- **Activity Cards 371, 372,** and **373** are appropriate for this lesson.
- Provide materials for weekly project. Gather newspaper and grocery ads or write a list of supplies and prices on the board.

NCTM Standards

Number and Operations Standard

Understand numbers, ways of representing numbers, relationships among numbers, and number systems

- understand the place-value structure of the base-ten number system and be able to represent and compare whole numbers and decimals;
- recognize and generate equivalent forms of commonly used fractions, decimals, and percents.

1 Fact Fluency

Hand out **Fact Fluency 27**. Remind students to color in the graph to show the number of correct answers and to set a goal for tomorrow.

2 Instruction

Decimals: Developing Meaning

- Write the number 573 on the board. Ask, *How can we write this number in expanded form?* (500 + 70 +3) Ask students to explain why we only need to write 5 in the number 573 instead of 500. If no one suggests that it is because of where the 5 is placed, write 453 on the board and say, *Does the 5 mean 500 in this number? Why not?* Help students understand that it is where the 5 is placed that changes its value. Write 5,238 on the board and ask, *What is the value of the 5 in this number?* (5,000)

- List the place names on the board from left to right: thousands, hundreds, tens, ones. Ask, *How many ones make 1 ten? How many tens make 1 hundred? How many hundreds make 1 thousand?* Ask, *What is the pattern?* (Each place is ten times greater than the place to its right.)

- Write 1,111.1 on the board. Ask, *What is different about this number?* (It has a decimal point.) Say, *Now let's write this number in expanded form.* Have children help as you write 1,000 + 100 + 10 + 1 + __. Point to the 1 in tenths place and say, *The value of this 1 should follow the same pattern—ten of them will make one.* Draw a square on the board and divide it into ten equal parts. Ask, *What is one part?* (One-tenth) *So the number 1,111.1 is 1,000 + 100 + 10 + 1 + $\frac{1}{10}$*

- Provide **Decimal Grids BLM 40,** crayons, scissors, and tape to students. Say, *These are ones squares that are magnified to make them bigger and easier to work with.* Ask, *How many small squares*

54

are in the ones squares? (100) Write 111.1 on the board. Have students work together to create 111.1 with the grids. Have them cut out 100 grids (you will need 8 copies of **Decimal Grids BLM 40**) and tape together to make a hundred square. Have them cut out 10 more grids and tape them together to make a ten stick. Have them cut out one grid for one. Have students color one vertical bar of 10 squares and cut it out to represent $\frac{1}{10}$. Tape all of these to the board to have a visual representation of 111.1.

- Say, *Let's check the pattern. Remember that every digit is ten times the digit to the right. Is 100 ten times 10? Is 10 ten times 1? Is 1 ten times $\frac{1}{10}$?* (yes to all) Say, *Notice that the decimal point separates the whole numbers from the fractions. When we read the number we say "and" when we get to the decimal point. This number is read as one hundred eleven and one-tenth.*

- Write 111.11 on the board and ask if someone could say the number. Ask, *How is this different from the one we taped to the board? What do we need to add to make this number?* ($\frac{1}{100}$) Have a student cut out $\frac{1}{100}$ of the decimal grid. Tape it to the board and change the number beneath to 111.11.

3 Kinesthetics

Decimal Dash

- Prepare place value areas of the room by labeling them as hundred, tens, ones, tenths, and hundredths. Say, *I will write a number. It may be a whole number or a decimal. When you see the number, think about it, then move to the place that represents its value.* Use numbers such as 500 (hundreds), 2 hundredths (0.02), thirty (tens), seven tenths (0.7), and so on.

- Repeat the activity by saying, rather than writing, numbers.

4 Studio Weekly Log

- Have each student work with a partner to complete page 2 of the **Studio Weekly Log**.

- Early Finishers: Provide appropriate **Activity Cards**.

5 Conversation

Have students check to see if each of their answers is reasonable. Then go over the answers together allowing students to share solution strategies and ask questions.

6 Math Game

Making Tenths

Play in groups of three or four. Each group will need a number decahedron and each student will need a copy of **Hundred Square BLM 10**. In turn, students will toss the number decahedron and shade in that number of hundredths. The object is to fill in complete columns to make tenths. Players can only shade in squares if there is that number of empty squares in a single column. For example, if a player tosses a 7, he or she can only shade in 7 squares in a single column; he or she cannot shade 3 squares in one column and 4 squares in another column. If there are not 7 squares in a single column, the player must wait until his or her next turn to toss again. After each round, students tell the decimal represented by their hundred square, such as 0.07. After 15 rounds, the student with the most squares filled in wins.

7 Weekly Project

Check progress and answer students' questions. Make sure students are all working with the correct amount of money. Remember to have the students look for healthy snacks, cups, plates, and napkins in the newspapers, or circulars. If the total price of "bought" items is larger than how much the students can spend, then they'll need to buy less expensive items.

8 Activity Cards

Provide appropriate cards for students to choose and complete. Remind students to record the number of completed cards in his/her **Studio Weekly Log**.

Comparing and Ordering Decimals

Knowledge and Skills

- Compare and order decimals in tenths and hundredths.

Preparation for Day 3

- Make copies, one per student:
  Fact Fluency 28
  Number Cards BLM 14 (Week 3)
  Decimal Grids BLM 40
- Obtain index cards or sheets of paper to prepare decimals cards for Kinesthetics.
- Take out safety scissors, counters, and crayons.
- **Activity Cards 374, 375,** and **376** are appropriate for this lesson.
- Display **Decimals** poster.
- Provide materials for weekly project.

NCTM Standards

Number and Operations Standard

Understand numbers, ways of representing numbers, relationships among numbers, and number systems

- understand the place-value structure of the base-ten number system and be able to represent and compare whole numbers and decimals;
- recognize and generate equivalent forms of commonly used fractions, decimals, and percents.

1 Fact Fluency

Hand out **Fact Fluency 28**. Remind students to color in the graph to show the number of correct answers and to set a goal for tomorrow.

2 Instruction

Equivalent Decimals: Developing Meaning

- Refer to the **Decimals** poster to review decimal fractions. Ask, *Which is a greater, 1 tenth or 1 hundredth?* (1 tenth). *How do you know?*

- Point to the square with $\frac{1}{10}$ shaded and ask, *What part of the whole is this?* ($\frac{1}{10}$) Ask, *How many tenths are there in 1 whole?* (10) Ask, *How do we write one-tenth as a decimal?* (0.1) Ask similar questions about the other shaded squares on the poster. Ask students to show two ways to write the last two examples on the poster. (0.10, 0.1; 0.50, 0.5)

- Distribute **Decimal Grids BLM 40** to each student. Have students color 27 hundredths on a decimal grid. Ask, *How many tenths are colored?* (2) *How many hundredths?* (7) Write 0.27 on the board. Say, *To write in expanded form we can write* $\frac{2}{10} + \frac{7}{100}$. Repeat with other similar examples as students shade grids and write on their decimal charts.

Comparing Decimals: Developing Meaning

- Ask, *Which number is greater, 0.32 or 0.4?* Have students color in two decimal grids and then explain why 0.4 is greater than 0.32. Ask, *What is another way to write 0.4?* ($\frac{4}{10}$, $\frac{40}{100}$, 0.40) Say, *It may be easier to compare decimals if you make them both hundredths because it is easier to see that 40 hundredths is greater than 32 hundredths.* Repeat with 2.03 and 2.3.

56

- List the following on the board and ask students to order them from least to greatest. 1.6, 1.06, 1.66, 1.61, 1.16, and 1.58. Have six students each color their grids to represent one of these numbers. Have them come to the front of the room and line up in order from least to greatest. Have each one tell his/her number and explain why she/he colored in the parts that they did. Have the rest of the class determine whether they are in the correct order. If anyone finds a mistake, ask that student to explain why.

3 Kinesthetics

Ordering Decimals

- Prepare cards with an assortment of decimals between 0 and 1. Examples include 0.0, 0.1, 0.5, 0.2, 0.22, 0.31, 0.36, 0.4, 0.40, 0.49, 0.50, 0.52, etc., to 1.0.

- Distribute the decimal cards randomly to students. Say, *I am going to give each person a card with a decimal number written on it. When I say GO, figure out how to arrange yourselves in order from least to greatest. If two decimals are equivalent, stand beside each other.*

- When students think they have formed themselves into the correct order, ask a volunteer to check the row and suggest any possible changes. Collect and shuffle the cards and repeat as time permits. Extend by using another deck with cards that include decimal numbers greater than 1. Keep these for Day 5.

4 Studio Weekly Log

- Have each student work with a partner to complete page 3 of the **Studio Weekly Log**.

- Early Finishers: Provide **Activity Cards**.

5 Conversation

Have students check to see if each of their answers is reasonable. Then go over the answers together allowing students to share solution strategies and ask questions.

6 Math Game

Decimal Chance

Play in pairs. Give each group a copy of **Number Cards BLM 14,** a pair of safety scissors, and a counter to serve as a decimal point. The object of the game is to form the greatest possible decimal number that has ones, tenths, and hundredths. Students draw one number card at a time. Once the card is drawn, the player positions it in any of the available open spaces in the 3-place number that will evolve. Once a card has been placed, it cannot be moved. This encourages students to think about the relative sizes of numbers and the chances of getting greater or smaller number in their next two draws. Whoever builds the greatest decimal in any round earns a point. Play continues until someone reaches 10 points.

7 Weekly Project

Check progress and answer students' questions. By now, students should have selected their menus and started working on their games.

8 Activity Cards

Provide appropriate cards for students to choose and complete. Remind students to record the number of completed cards in his/her **Studio Weekly Log**.

Adding and Subtracting Decimals with Manipulatives

Knowledge and Skills

- Develop strategies for adding and subtracting decimals using manipulatives.

Preparation for Day 4

- Make copies, one per student:
  Fact Fluency 29
  Decimal Grids BLM 40
  Making Half Grid BLM 41
- Take the number decahedrons from the kit. (Math Game)
- **Activity Cards 380, 381,** and **383** are appropriate for this lesson.
- Provide materials for weekly project.

NCTM Standards

Number and Operations Standard

Understand numbers, ways of representing numbers, relationships among numbers, and number systems

- understand the place-value structure of the base-ten number system and be able to represent and compare whole numbers and decimals.

Compute fluently and make reasonable estimates

- develop and use strategies to estimate computations involving fractions and decimals;
- use visual models, benchmarks, and equivalent forms to add and subtract commonly used fractions and decimals.

1 Fact Fluency

Hand out **Fact Fluency 29**. Remind students to color in the graph to show the number of correct answers and to set a goal for tomorrow.

2 Instruction

Adding and Subtracting Decimals: Developing Strategies

- Distribute copies of **Decimal Grids BLM 40**. Remind students to think of each square as 1 whole. Ask *How many wholes are on this page?* (15) *How would we write this amount as a decimal?* (15.0 or 15.00) *How would we write it if it were an amount of money?* ($15.00)
- Have students look at the first square and shade 0.45 of it. Ask, *Is this more or less than half of the square.* (less than half) Have students color in 0.32 on the same grid. Ask, *What is the sum of 0.45 and 0.32?* Make sure that students are saying the answer correctly—in this case, zero and seventy-seven hundredths.
- Write 0.45 + 0.32 on the board in vertical form. Model adding without using the grids.
- Write 0.3 + 0.03 on the board. Ask students to read each addend aloud. Have a student model writing this addition in vertical form. Say, *Just as with whole numbers, you align numbers that have the same place value.* Repeat with other examples for students to shade and add.
- Model addition with decimals greater than one. Write 1.35 + 2.24 on the board. Say, *Estimate what whole numbers the answer will be between. Explain how you know.* (more than 3 and less than 4)
- Write it in vertical form and have students help you find the sum. Say, *What is 1 plus 2?* (3) *What is three-tenths plus 2 tenths?* (5 tenths) *What is five hundredths plus four hundredths?* (9 hundredths)

58

What is the sum? (3.59; three and fifty-nine hundredths) Ask, *Was our estimation that the answer would be between 3 and 4 correct? Is the answer greater or less than $3\frac{1}{2}$?* (greater) *How do you know?* Repeat with other examples, but avoid regrouping.

- Ask volunteers to explain how they could use the grids to subtract decimals. Possible ideas include drawing a border around the greater decimal number, then crossing out squares to show the amount to be subtracted.

- On the board, write $0.86 - 0.41$. Have students solve it on a grid. (0.45) Ask, *Is this answer greater or less than half?* (less) Model the subtraction in vertical form. Repeat with other examples, including decimals greater than 1. Again, avoid the need to regroup.

3 Kinesthetics

Decimal Action

- Have students stand around the room and do a few warm-up stretches.

- Say, *I will write a decimal on the board. On my signal, you will clap the number of hundredths in the decimal and jump the number of tenths in the decimal. For example, if I write 0.54, you will clap 4 times and jump 5 times. Then I will write another decimal on the board and you will clap the number of hundredths and jump the number of tenths. Then I will tell you to add or subtract the two decimals and you will clap the number of tenths in the answer and jump the number of hundredths in the answer.*

- Choose decimals less than 1 that are in tenths or hundredths. Avoid numbers that will require regrouping. Write the answer to each exercise on the board after the students have acted it out.

4 Studio Weekly Log

- Have each student work with a partner to complete page 4 of the **Studio Weekly Log**.

- Early Finishers: Provide appropriate **Activity Cards**.

5 Conversation

Have students check to see if each of their answers is reasonable. Then go over the answers together allowing students to share solution strategies and ask questions.

6 Math Game

Making Half

Play in groups of three or four. Give each student a copy of **Making Half Grid BLM 41**. Players take turns tossing a number decahedron with numbers 0–9. The number each player tosses must be written into the grid as tenths (0, 0.1, 0.2, and so on). Students can add or subtract across the row to make one half. For example, if a student tosses a 4, he or she would write 0.4 in the grid. He or she would need to toss a 1 to complete that row, since $0.4 + 0.1 = 0.5$. If a student tosses a 7, he or she would write 0.7 in the grid. He or she would need to toss a 2 to complete that row, since $0.7 - 0.2 = 0.5$. If a number is tossed that cannot be written in the grid, that student must wait for his/her next turn to toss again. Whoever completes their grid first, wins.

7 Weekly Project

Check progress and answer students' questions. Today they should finish their menus and prepare to present their games to the class.

8 Activity Cards

Provide appropriate cards for students to choose and complete. Remind students to record the number of completed cards in his/her **Studio Weekly Log**.

Estimating with Decimals

Knowledge and Skills

- Understand and apply decimal concepts to rounding and estimating.

Preparation for Day 5

- Make copies, one per student:
  Fact Fluency 30
  Decimals in Sports BLM 42
  Decimal Number Lines BLM 43
  Six-Week Cumulative Assessment
- Use Decimal Cards from Day 3 for Kinesthics.
- **Activity Card 384** is appropriate for this lesson.

NCTM Standards

Number and Operations Standard

Understand numbers, ways of representing numbers, relationships among numbers, and number systems

- develop understanding of fractions as parts of unit wholes, as parts of a collection, as locations on number lines, and as divisions of whole numbers.

Compute fluently and make reasonable estimates

- develop and use strategies to estimate computations involving fractions and decimals in situations relevant to students' experience.

1 Fact Fluency

Hand out **Fact Fluency 30**. Remind students to shade in the graph to show the number of correct answers.

2 Instruction

- Revisit the essential question posed on Day 1 (What is the meaning of a decimal point?). Invite students to respond in their own words with examples from their experience and from this week's work.

- Distribute **Decimals in Sports BLM 42**. Ask questions about the decimals shown on the BLM. Examples include *Which decimal is a little more than 30?* (30.1) *Which decimal is a little less than 9?* (8.95)

- Hand out copies of **Decimal Number Line BLM 43**. Explain that this page contains some blank number lines. Model numbering the first line so that it goes from 0.0 to 1.0 by tenths.

- Say, *Put your finger on the number that is halfway between zero and one. What number is it?* (five tenths) Ask, *Is three tenths nearer to zero or to one?* (zero) Ask similar questions for 0.6 and 0.8. Then point out that any decimal greater than 0.0 but less than 0.5 is nearer to zero, while any decimal greater than 0.5 nearer to 1.

- Have students label the next number line in tenths from 4.0 to 5.0. As they are doing this, write the following addition on the board in vertical form: 2.1 + 2.1.

- Say, *Suppose we added these two numbers. Would the sum be nearer to 4 or to 5? How do you know?* (4) Have students add the numbers mentally. Ask a volunteer to explain how he/she added them mentally. Have students locate the sum (4.2) on the number line. Ask *Is it closer to 4 or 5?* Repeat with several other examples.

- Say, *Margot went to the store and bought two packages of cheese at the deli. One piece weighed 1.3 pounds and the other weighed 0.8 pounds.* Ask, *Did she buy more or less than 2 pounds of cheese?* Explain your thinking.

- Say, *Jose bought two pieces of fish. The trout weighed 1.98 lb. The salmon weighed 2.0 lb. Which weighed more?* (the salmon) Have students explain or model how they know.

3 Kinesthetics

Give each student a card with a decimal number on it saved from Day 3. (The numbers should range from 0.4 to 3.5.) Say, *I am going to say a number such as 4 and you are to find someone to pair up with so that the sum of your numbers is close to 4.* Repeat using different numbers. You may want to say a number such as 10 and have more than two students get together to make a sum close to 10.

4 Studio Weekly Log

- Have each student work with a partner to complete page 5 of the **Studio Weekly Log**.

- Early Finishers: Provide appropriate **Activity Cards**.

5 Conversation

Have students check to see if each of their answers is reasonable. Then go over the answers together allowing students to share solution strategies and ask questions.

6 Assessment

Have students complete.

7 Weekly Project

Have pairs take turns presenting their party plans to each other. Have students play each game, as time permits. Encourage active participation, questioning, and discussion.

8 Family Letter

Have students turn to the back cover of their **Studio Weekly Log**. Tell students to write a letter to their family about what they learned in math class this week.

Your kit includes enough cards so that each student can have one Reward Card per week. Simply punch out the desired number of cards that match the riddle that is on the cover of the **Studio Weekly Log** for that week and distribute them to your students.

Blackline Masters

- **Fact Fluencies**
- **Pre-Test**
- **Weekly Assessments**
- **Cumulative Assessment**
- **Manipulatives**
- **Projects**
- **Post-Test**
- **Worksheets**

Name _______________________________

Date _______________________________

1 Write as decimals:

a $\frac{4}{10}$ = _____ **b** $\frac{39}{100}$ = _____ **c** $\frac{7}{10}$ = _____ **d** $\frac{56}{100}$ = _____

2 Write as fractions:

a 0.12 = _____ **b** 0.6 = _____ **c** 0.09 = _____ **d** 0.85 = _____

3 Circle the greater number:

a $\frac{4}{100}$, 0.40 **b** 0.02, 8 out of 100 **c** $\frac{68}{100}$, 49 hundredths

4 Write in order from least to greatest:

0.49   0.25   0.06   0.98   0.17

_______ _______ _______ _______ _______

5 On this number line show:

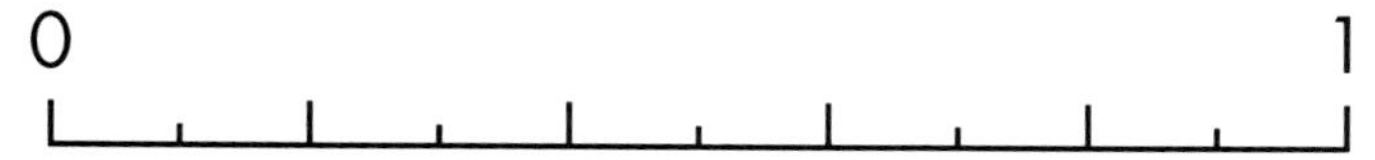

a $\frac{2}{10}$ on top, 0.2 on the bottom.

b $\frac{7}{10}$ on top, 0.7 on the bottom.

c $\frac{3}{5}$ on top, 0.6 on the bottom.

6 Add or subtract.

a 1.1 + 2.6 = _________

b 4.5 + 5.2 = _________

c 8.3 − 4.2 = _________

7 Daryl lives 36.4 miles from his grandfather. Which whole mile is nearest to that distance?

○ **a** 35   ○ **b** 36   ○ **c** 37

Name _______________________________

Date _______________________________

8 Write in numerals:
a four hundred thirty

____

b six hundred twelve

____

9 Draw lines to show eighths. Shade $\frac{1}{2}$.

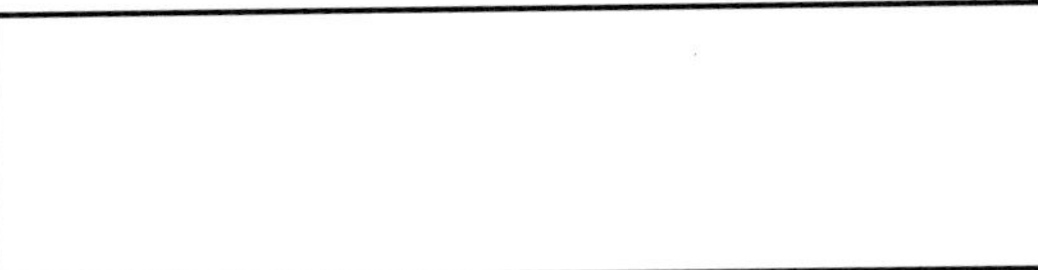

10 46 + 19 = _______

11 $\begin{array}{r} 78 \\ -26 \\ \hline \end{array}$ $\begin{array}{r} 55 \\ -13 \\ \hline \end{array}$ $\begin{array}{r} 89 \\ -10 \\ \hline \end{array}$

12 Carlos worked for 4 hours and earned \$6 per hour. How much did he earn in all? _______

13 $\begin{array}{r} 8 \\ \times 5 \\ \hline \end{array}$ $\begin{array}{r} 6 \\ \times 3 \\ \hline \end{array}$ $\begin{array}{r} 7 \\ \times 2 \\ \hline \end{array}$ $\begin{array}{r} 9 \\ \times 5 \\ \hline \end{array}$

14 Shade to match the fraction.

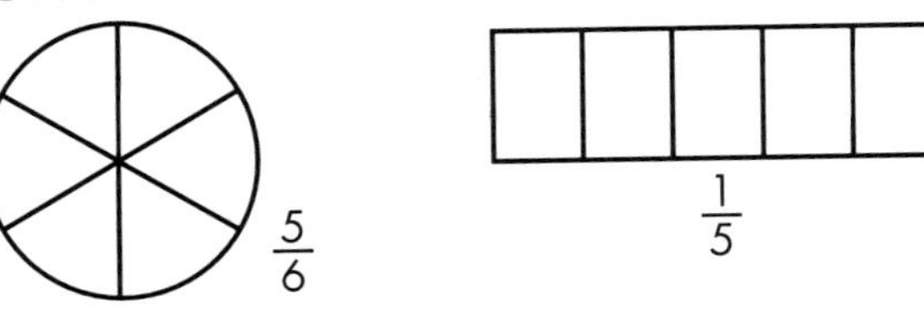

15 What is:
a $\frac{1}{8}$ of 16 flowers? _______
b $\frac{1}{5}$ of 25 grapes? _______

16 Count backwards by 5s:
40 _______ _______ _______

17 a 48 ÷ 8 = _______

b 14 ÷ 7 = _______

18 What number is halfway between 1 and 2? _______

19 Brooke bought two packages of cheese from the Deli. One weighed 0.3 pounds and the other weighed 0.5 pounds. Did she buy more or less than 1 pound of cheese? _______

20 Which number is a multiple of 6?
a 12 **b** 15 **c** 20

Fact Fluency
1

Name _______________________________

Write numbers.

1 less than:	10 more than:	10 less than:
1 40 _______	**6** 20 _______	**11** 80 _______
2 78 _______	**7** 50 _______	**12** 30 _______
3 14 _______	**8** 6 _______	**13** 71 _______
4 51 _______	**9** 56 _______	**14** 20 _______
5 99 _______	**10** 15 _______	**15** 96 _______

▶ Fill in the graph to show how many you did correctly in one minute.

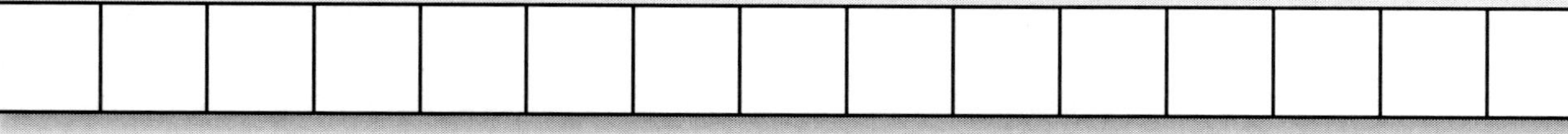

1	2	3	4	5	6	7	8	9	10	11	12	13	14	15

My goal for tomorrow is:______
(Write in the number you want to get correct tomorrow.)

Making Tens

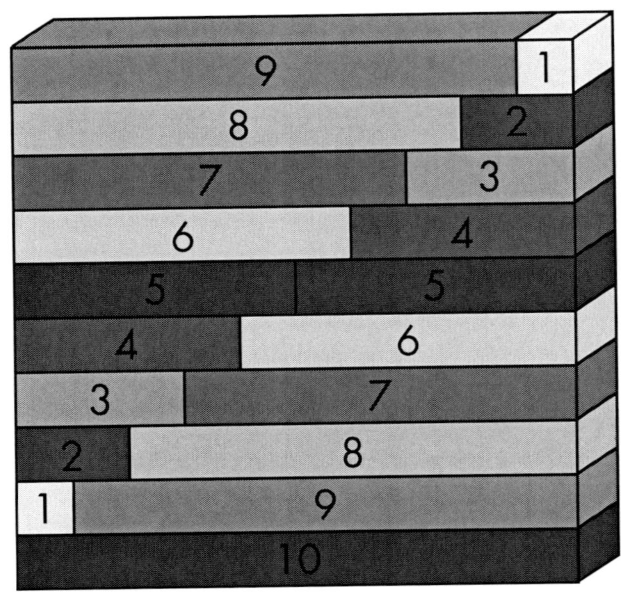

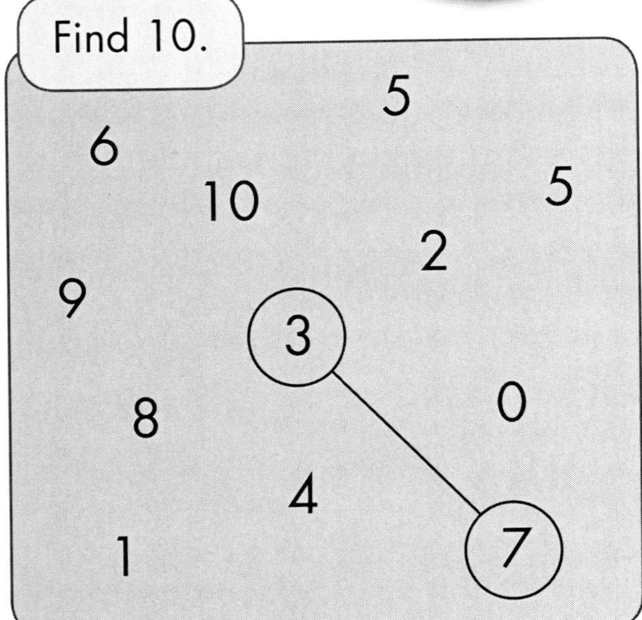

4	8	2	4	1	5	7
10	0	5	9	5	6	3
8	5	6	8	3	10	4
9	1	4	2	7	0	3

Challenge! Loop three numbers which add to 10.

Making Tens Grid

BLM 2

toss	+	toss	=	10
	+		=	10
	+		=	10
	+		=	10
	+		=	10
	+		=	10

toss	+	toss	=	10
	+		=	10
	+		=	10
	+		=	10
	+		=	10
	+		=	10

toss	+	toss	=	10
	+		=	10
	+		=	10
	+		=	10
	+		=	10
	+		=	10

The Snack Store 

Work with your partner to plan a snack store that will sell healthy lunch snacks for the class.

Part 1
- Make a list of healthy snack foods and drinks.
- Show your list to 3 or 4 other students for their suggestions.
- Make your final list of snacks for your store.

Part 2
- Choose a name for your store.
- Decide on prices for each snack on your list.
- Make a menu or a sign for your snack store.
- List your snacks from the most expensive to the least expensive.

Part 3
- Use the money from the kit and take turns being the customer and the store clerk.
- When you are the customer, you get 2 one-dollar bills to spend. Select the snacks you want to buy.
- Your partner will tell you the total amount to pay. You will pay and your partner will give you the proper change.
- Make a chart to record each customer's purchases. Here is an example.

Name of customer	Snacks purchased	Total bill	Change from $1.00
Shawn	Bean Soup 45¢ Vegetable juice 25¢	70¢	30¢
Felicia	Fruit Salad 75¢ Whole-wheat roll 15¢	90¢	10¢

Fact Fluency 2

Name _______________________________

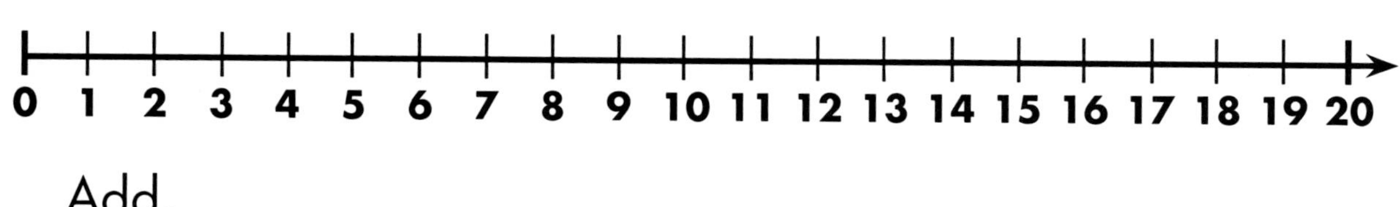

Add.

1 $7 + 9 =$ ______	**9** $12 + 7 =$ ______
2 $6 + 5 =$ ______	**10** $8 + 9 =$ ______
3 $10 + 8 =$ ______	**11** $9 + 6 =$ ______
4 $4 + 5 =$ ______	**12** $3 + 9 =$ ______
5 $5 + 9 =$ ______	**13** $11 + 7 =$ ______
6 $6 + 8 =$ ______	**14** $7 + 7 =$ ______
7 $8 + 3 =$ ______	**15** $2 + 7 =$ ______
8 $4 + 8 =$ ______	

▶ Fill in the graph to show how many you did correctly in one minute.

My goal for tomorrow is:______
(Write in the number you want to get correct tomorrow.)

Place-Value Grids

Hundreds	Tens	Ones

Hundreds	Tens	Ones

Fact Fluency 3

Name _______________________________

Add.

1 15 + 5 = _______

2 12 + 3 = _______

3 16 + 4 = _______

4 18 + 1 = _______

5 11 + 9 = _______

6 15 + 10 = _______

7 18 + 10 = _______

8 10 + 10 = _______

9 25 + 10 = _______

10 1 + 10 = _______

11 73 + 10 = _______

12 14 + 10 = _______

13 80 + 10 = _______

14 9 + 3 = _______

15 8 + 7 = _______

▶ Fill in the graph to show how many you did correctly in one minute.

1	2	3	4	5	6	7	8	9	10	11	12	13	14	15

My goal for tomorrow is: _______
(Write in the number you want to get correct tomorrow.)

Number Expanders

Ones Tens Hundreds

Ones Tens Hundreds

Ones Tens Hundreds

Ones Tens Hundreds

Ones Tens Hundreds

Fact Fluency 4

Name ___________________________________

Write each number.

1 one hundred forty-two

____

2 two hundred fifteen

____

3 eight hundred seventy-three

____

4 five hundred twenty-nine

____

5 six hundred four

____

6 nine hundred nineteen

____

7 four hundred fifty

____

8 seven hundred thirty-eight

____

Write in order from least to greatest.

9 218, 715, 175

_______ _______ _______

10 301, 97, 258

_______ _______ _______

11 592, 903, 487

_______ _______ _______

12 650, 599, 711

_______ _______ _______

13 281, 812, 182

_______ _______ _______

14 917, 971, 791

_______ _______ _______

15 203, 230, 302

_______ _______ _______

▶ Fill in the graph to show how many you did correctly in one minute.

1	**2**	**3**	**4**	**5**	**6**	**7**	**8**	**9**	**10**	**11**	**12**	**13**	**14**	**15**

My goal for tomorrow is:_______
(Write in the number you want to get correct tomorrow.)

Name ___________________________

Add.

1 $7 + 3 =$ _____

2 $47 + 3 =$ _____

3 $5 + 5 =$ _____

4 $65 + 5 =$ _____

5 $4 + 6 =$ _____

6 $34 + 6 =$ _____

7 $9 + 1 =$ _____

8 $89 + 1 =$ _____

9 $8 + 2 =$ _____

10 $58 + 2 =$ _____

11 $3 + 7 =$ _____

12 $73 + 7 =$ _____

13 $6 + 4 + 8 =$ _____

14 $5 + 7 + 5 =$ _____

15 $9 + 2 + 8 =$ _____

▶ Fill in the graph to show how many you did correctly in one minute.

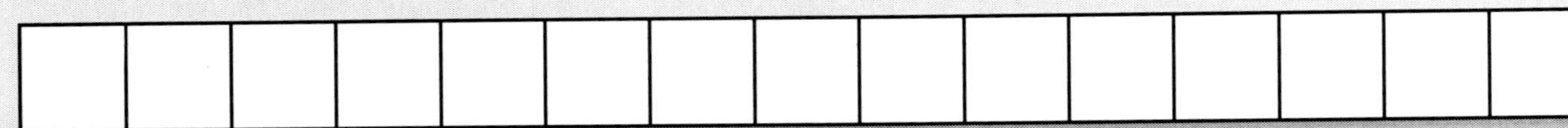

Number Lines

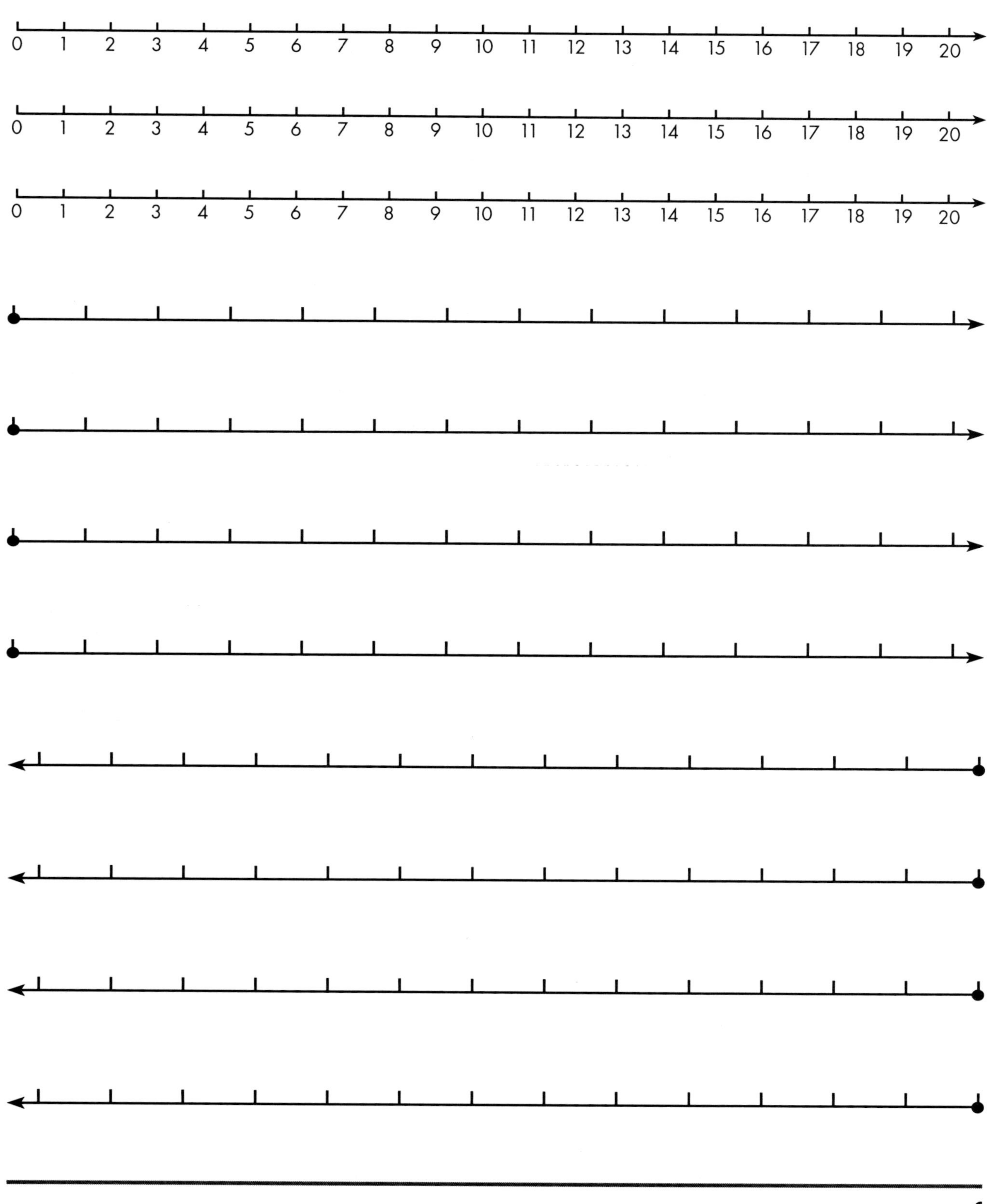

Name ___________________________

Date ___________________________

1 Write the number.

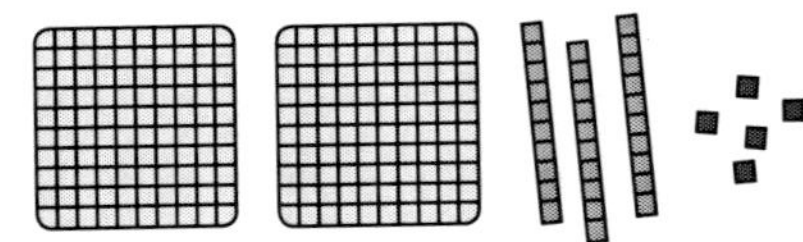 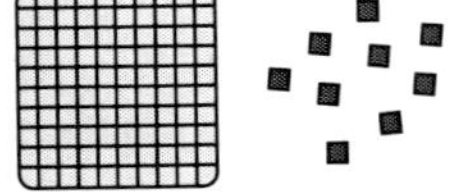

a ___________________ **b** ___________________

2 Write in order. Start with the least number.

___________   ___________   ___________   ___________

3 What belongs in the box?

a 961 = ☐ + 60 + 1 **c** 300 + 40 + ☐ = 342

b 28 = 400 + ☐ + 8 **d** 500 + ☐ + 7 = 507

4 Write each number.

a fifty-six _______ **b** two hundred nineteen _______

5 Solve.

a 6 + 5 = _______ **b** 8 + 4 = _______ **c** 7 + 3 = _______

6 Round these numbers to the nearest ten.

a 26 _______ **b** 13 _______ **c** 92 _______ **d** 59 _______

7 Which of the following is more than 50?

○ **a** 12 + 43 ○ **b** 15 + 18 ○ **c** 20 + 22

Fact Fluency 6

Name ___________________________________

Add.

1 6 + 7 = ________

2 5 + 4 = ________

3 8 + 9 = ________

4 11 + 10 = ________

5 4 + 3 = ________

6 12 + 7 = ________

7 14 + 9 + 6 = ________

8 22 + 9 + 8 = ________

9 8 + 12 + 15 = ________

10 5 + 6 + 25 = ________

11 11 + 17 + 3 = ________

12 17 + 6 + 4 = ________

13 15 + 9 + 15 = ________

14 19 + 8 + 11 = ________

15 21 + 9 + 7 = ________

▶ Fill in the graph to show how many you did correctly in one minute.

1	2	3	4	5	6	7	8	9	10	11	12	13	14	15

My goal for tomorrow is: _______
(Write in the number you want to get correct tomorrow.)

Operation Wheels

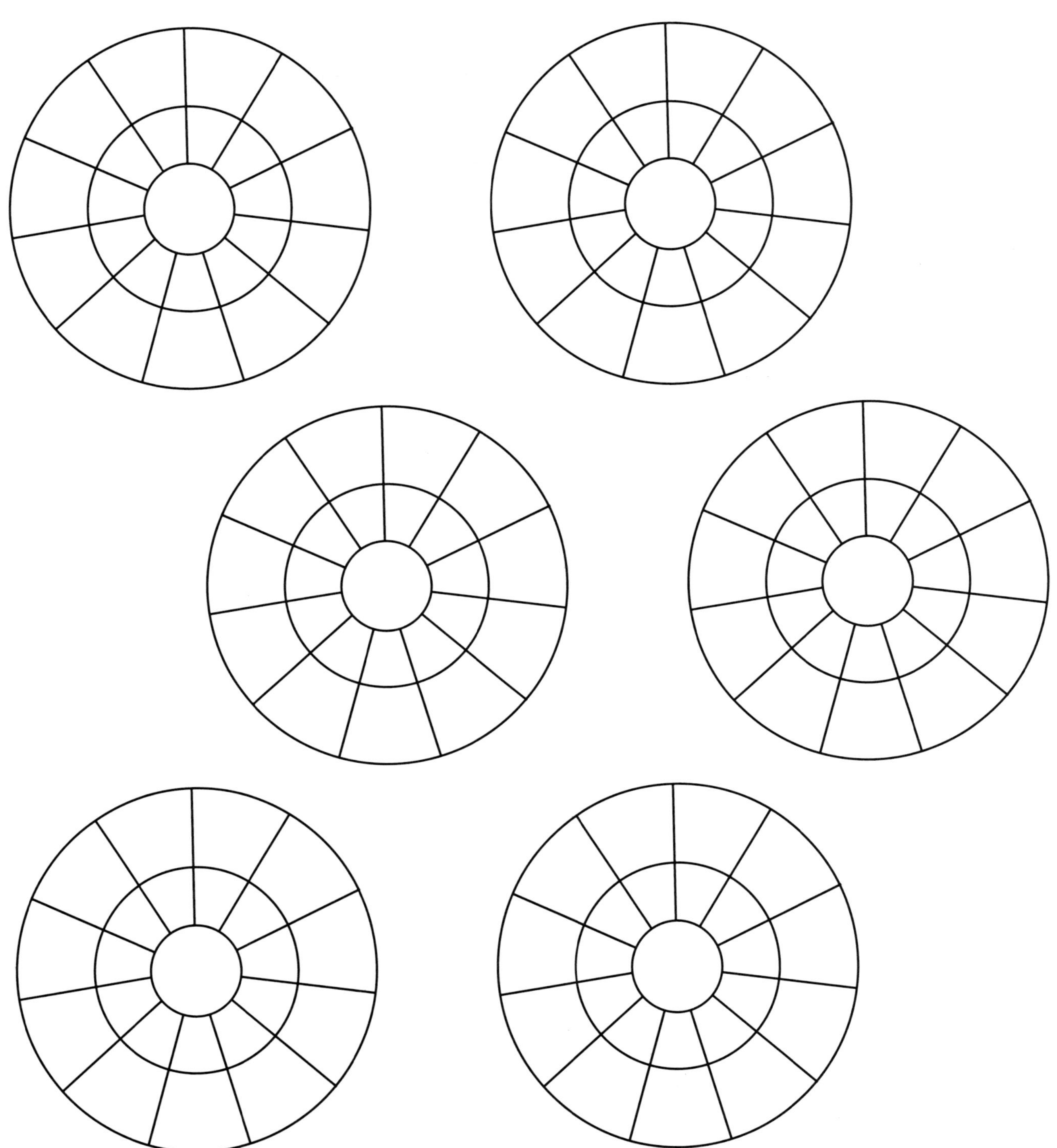

Animal Giants

Imagine an animal giant, such as a dinosaur or giant squid.

Part 1

- Decide how tall and heavy your giant is. Draw your giant.
- Compare the height and weight of your giant with the animal giants listed below. Is your animal taller, shorter, heavier, or lighter? Find the differences.

Part 2

- Create a schedule for your giant. Include things like looking for food, eating, sleeping, and playing.
- Plan a plane trip for you and your giant. Think about what other animals you could invite. NOTE: The plane can only carry 30,000 pounds and its cabin is only 7 feet tall.

Part 3

Write word problems about your animal with addition and subtraction situations.

Animal Giant	Height	Weight
Hippopotamus	5 feet	10,000 pounds
Elephant	13 feet	14,000 pounds
Tyrannosaurus Rex	39 feet	20,000 pounds
Giant Squid	59 feet	2,000 pounds

Name _______________________________

Add.

1 16 + 11 = _______ **9** 14 + 16 = _______

2 14 + 12 = _______ **10** 11 + 17 = _______

3 17 + 10 = _______ **11** 18 + 15 = _______

4 15 + 14 = _______ **12** 14 + 14 = _______

5 18 + 13 = _______ **13** 12 + 16 = _______

6 12 + 12 = _______ **14** 17 + 12 = _______

7 13 + 15 = _______ **15** 15 + 12 = _______

8 19 + 13 = _______

▶ Fill in the graph to show how many you did correctly in one minute.

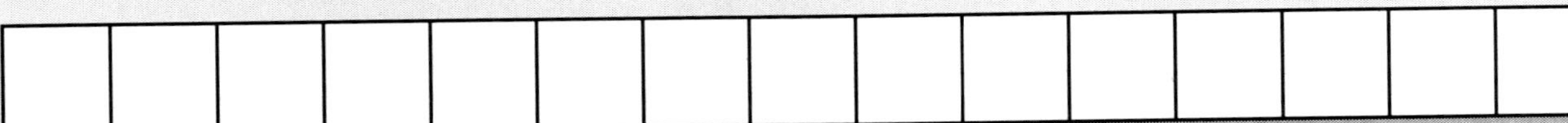

1	2	3	4	5	6	7	8	9	10	11	12	13	14	15

My goal for tomorrow is: _______
(Write in the number you want to get correct tomorrow.)

Part-Part-Whole

Part	Part
Whole	

Name _______________________________

Complete.

1 $6 + 8 - 7 =$ _______

2 $11 - 4 + 5 =$ _______

3 $3 + 8 - 4 =$ _______

4 $17 - 9 + 5 =$ _______

5 $15 - 5 + 6 =$ _______

6 $8 + 5 - 6 =$ _______

7 $13 - 4 + 9 =$ _______

8 $9 + 7 - 5 =$ _______

9 $20 - 12 + 8 =$ _______

10 $4 + 9 - 8 =$ _______

11 $10 + 6 - 12 =$ _______

12 $14 - 6 + 11 =$ _______

13 $5 + 7 - 4 =$ _______

14 $16 - 4 + 7 =$ _______

15 $6 + 6 - 2 =$ _______

▶ Fill in the graph to show how many you did correctly in one minute.

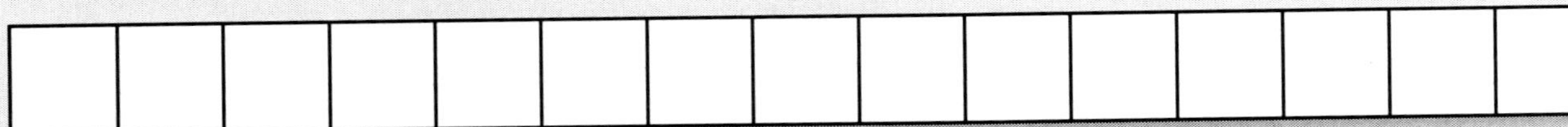

My goal for tomorrow is:______
(Write in the number you want to get correct tomorrow.)

Name _______________________________________

Subtract.

1 16 − 7 = _______   **9** 11 − 3 = _______

2 12 − 4 = _______   **10** 16 − 5 = _______

3 20 − 9 = _______   **11** 12 − 9 = _______

4 13 − 7 = _______   **12** 17 − 8 = _______

5 18 − 9 = _______   **13** 14 − 5 = _______

6 15 − 6 = _______   **14** 16 − 9 = _______

7 12 − 8 = _______   **15** 19 − 12 = _______

8 14 − 7 = _______

▶ Fill in the graph to show how many you did correctly in one minute.

1	2	3	4	5	6	7	8	9	10	11	12	13	14	15

My goal for tomorrow is:______
(Write in the number you want to get correct tomorrow.)

Hundreds Square

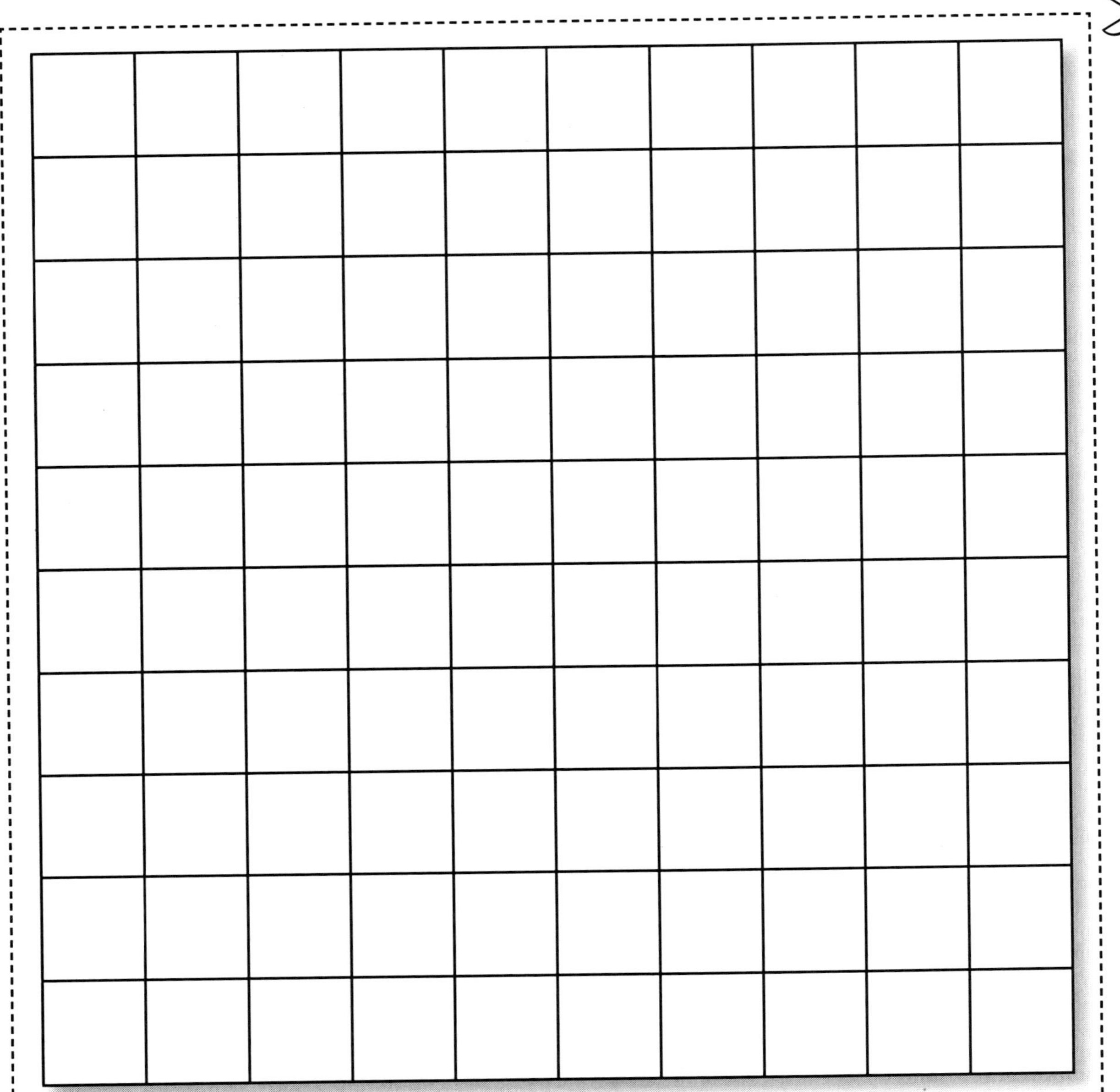

Tens Rods

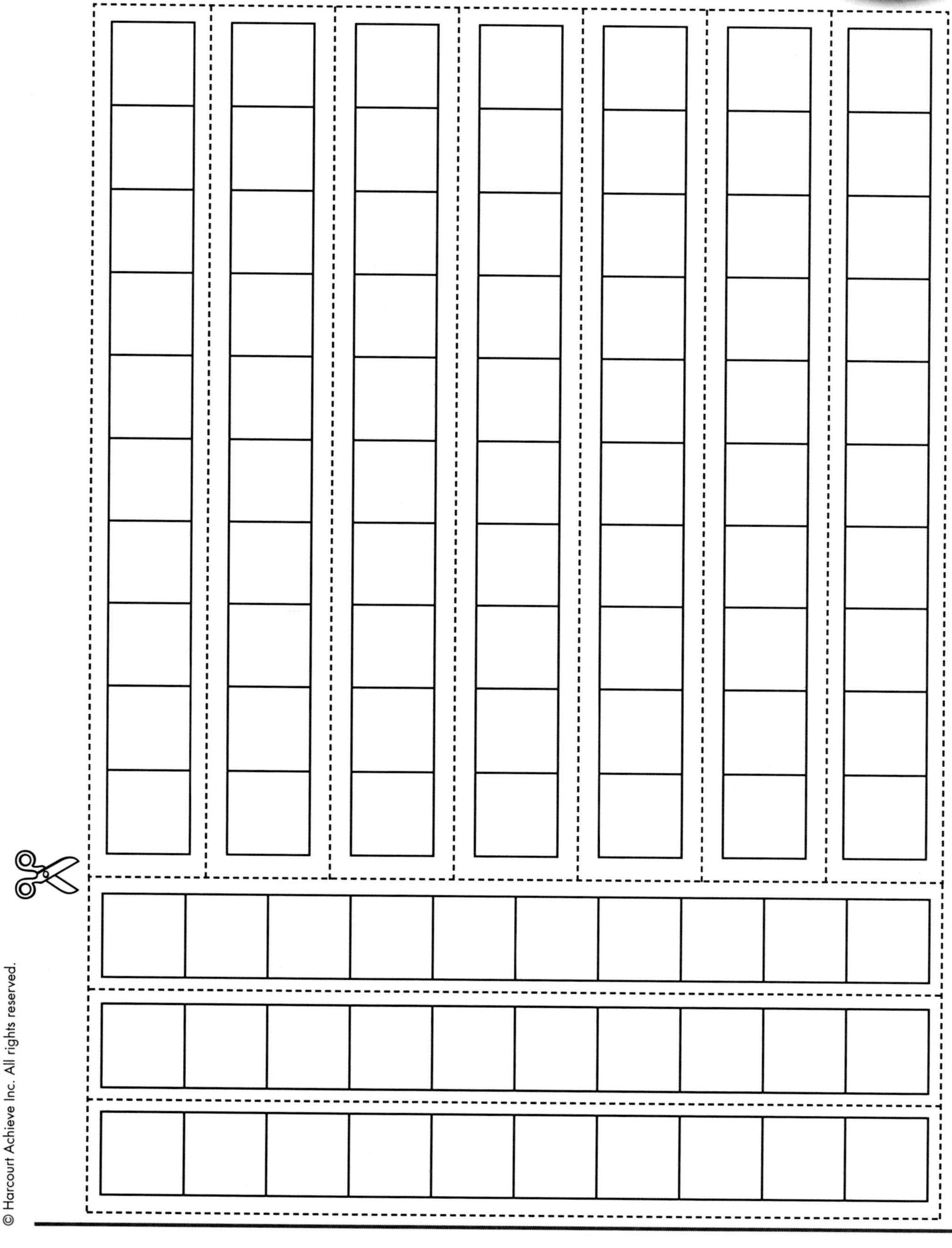

Unit Squares

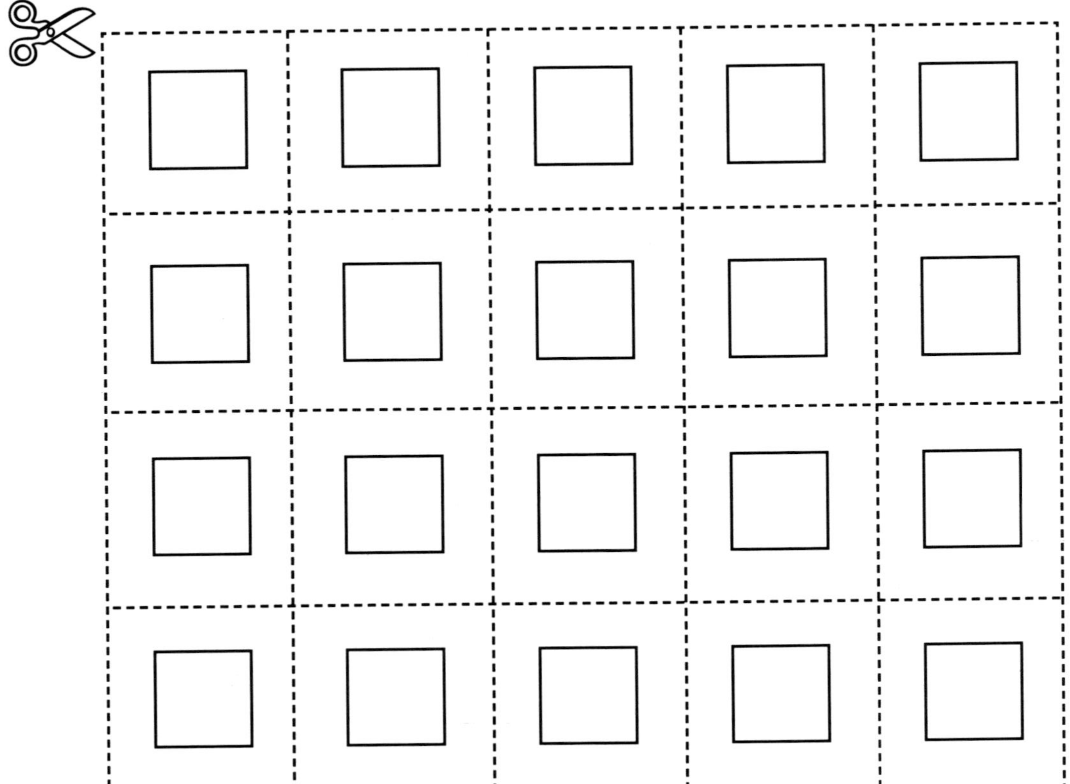

Name ______________________________

Add.

1 16 + 19 = ________   **9** 41 + 37 = ________

2 42 + 18 = ________   **10** 37 + 17 = ________

3 27 + 29 = ________   **11** 19 + 38 = ________

4 24 + 28 = ________   **12** 14 + 49 = ________

5 39 + 19 = ________   **13** 23 + 18 = ________

6 25 + 39 = ________   **14** 38 + 29 = ________

7 18 + 19 = ________   **15** 35 + 17 = ________

8 45 + 28 = ________

▶ Fill in the graph to show how many you did correctly in one minute.

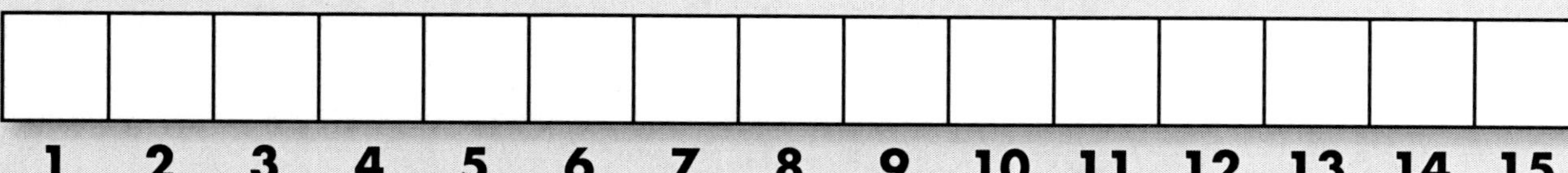

Name _______________________________

Date _______________________________

0   10   20   30   40   50   60   70   80   90   100

1 Find the total. Use the number line.

a $9 + 7 + 1 =$ _____   **d** $8 + 2 + 6 =$ _____   **g** $31 + 25 =$ _____

b $43 + 19 =$ _____   **e** $52 + 27 =$ _____   **h** $23 - 5 =$ _____

c $64 + 8 =$ _____   **f** $18 - 9 =$ _____   **i** $34 - 27 =$ _____

2 Complete. Draw base ten blocks to show your regrouping.

a $168 + 49 =$ _____

b $256 - 108 =$ _____

3 The green lizard is 35 inches long. The brown lizard is 26 inches long. What is the difference?

○ **a** 8 inches   ○ **b** 9 inches   ○ **c** 10 inches   ○ **d** 11 inches

Name ___________________________________

Subtract.

1	16 − 7 = _______	**9**	11 − 3 = _______
2	12 − 4 = _______	**10**	16 − 5 = _______
3	20 − 9 = _______	**11**	12 − 9 = _______
4	13 − 7 = _______	**12**	17 − 8 = _______
5	18 − 9 = _______	**13**	14 − 5 = _______
6	15 − 6 = _______	**14**	16 − 9 = _______
7	12 − 8 = _______	**15**	19 − 12 = _______
8	14 − 7 = _______		

▶ Fill in the graph to show how many you did correctly in one minute.

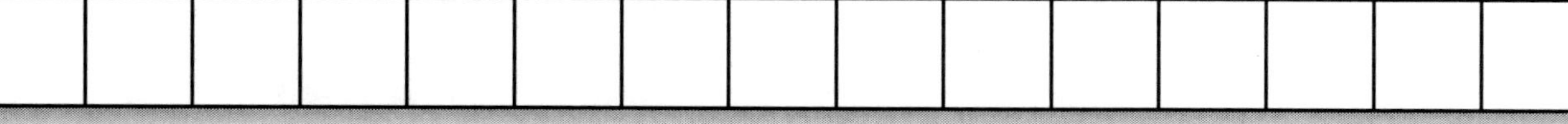

1	2	3	4	5	6	7	8	9	10	11	12	13	14	15

My goal for tomorrow is:______
(Write in the number you want to get correct tomorrow.)

Multiplication

On a separate sheet of paper, write an addition sentence for each group. Then write a multiplication sentence.
For example: a. $3 + 3 + 3 = 9$ and $3 \times 3 = 9$.

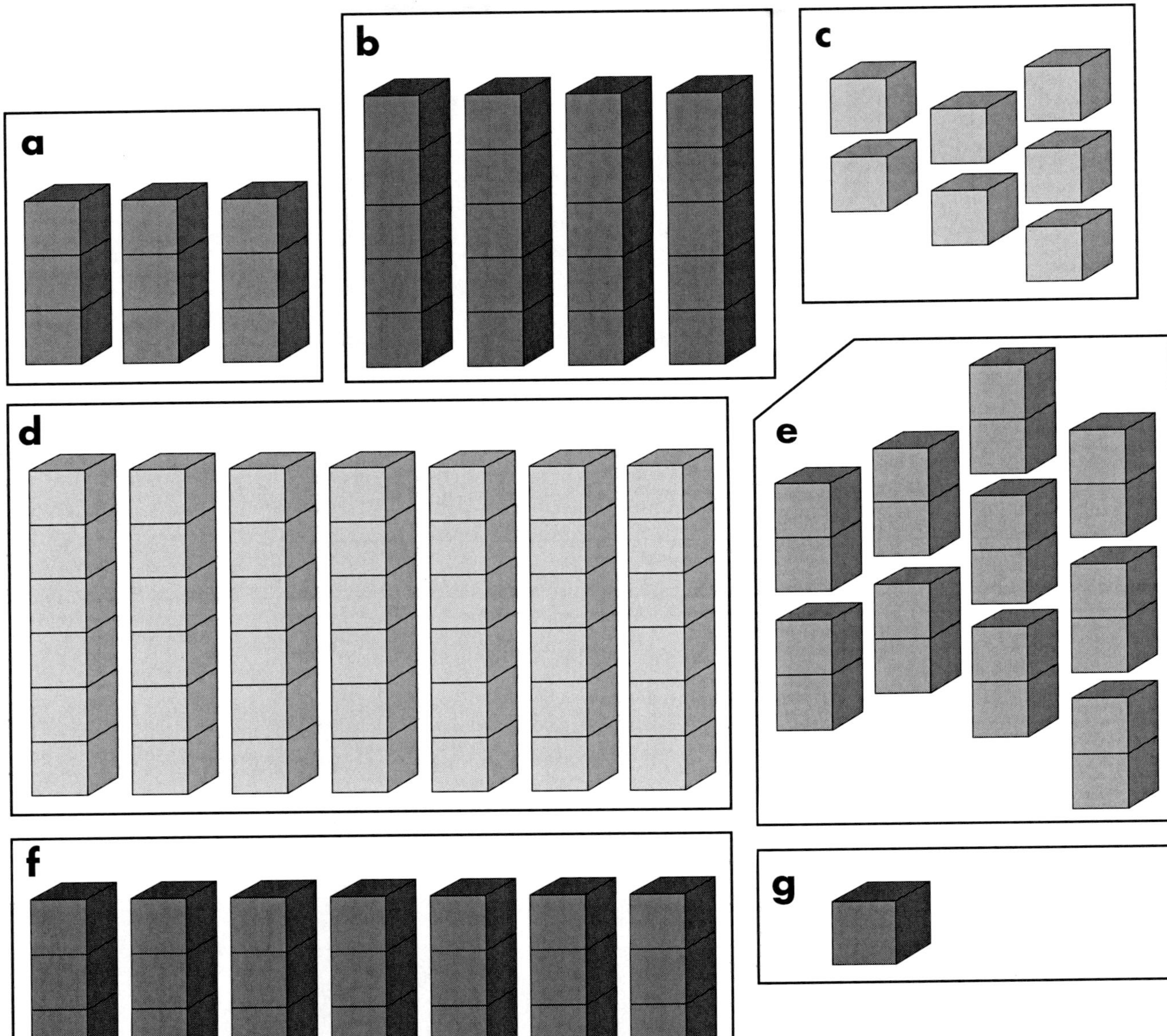

Number Cards

0	**1**	**2**
3	**4**	**5**
6	**7**	**8**
9	**10**	**✕**

WEEK **THREE**

Creepy, Crawly Math

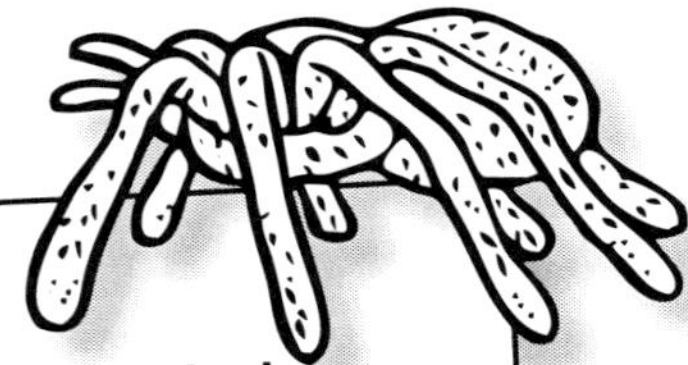

You will research, plan, and write math problems for a quiz show.

Part 1
• Think about the many creatures that creep, crawl, hop, swim, or fly. Write some interesting facts about these creatures that involve numbers. Use **Creepy, Crawly, Hoppy Number Facts BLM 16** for more ideas.
• Draw or find pictures of some of the creatures. Include groups of the creatures in your drawings so that you can use them to write multiplication questions.

Part 2
• Choose a name and make up rules for your quiz show. Plan a scoring system for players to earn (or lose) points.
• Assign jobs. You will need a question reader, a judge, and a scorekeeper. You may also need a time keeper.

Part 3
• Write ten quiz show questions with answers. Write some questions that need multiplication to solve. For example, *A toad has 4 legs. How many legs would there be on 6 toads?*
• On Friday, conduct your math quiz show.

Creepy, Crawly, Hoppy Number Facts

Here are some interesting facts about animals. You may use the facts to write quiz show questions. You can also look for other cool facts.

- A snake has 0 legs.
- A banana slug has only 1 foot.
- A praying mantis has only 1 ear.
- A spider has 8 legs.
- A caterpillar has 2 rows of eyes.
- Coccinella is a ladybug that has 7 spots.
- A tarantula has 8 legs.
- An octopus has 8 tentacles (arms). So does a squid.
- An insect has 6 legs.
- An armadillo has 9 bands of "armor" on its back.
- A grasshopper has 4 wings.
- A crab has 10 legs.
- A snail has 2 antennae.
- A termite has 2 pincers.
- A wasp has 3 eyes.
- Insect bodies have 3 parts.
- A cicada has 4 wings.
- A female firefly has no wings.
- Alligators have 4 toes on each back foot.
- A scorpion's tail has 5 sections.
- Most starfish have 5 arms.
- An ant has 6 legs.
- A cricket has 7 breathing holes.

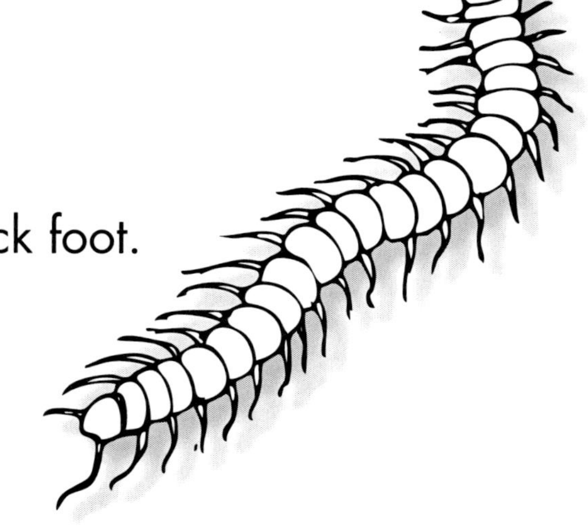

Name _______________________________

Solve.

1 $6 + 8 - 7 =$ _______ **4** $17 - 9 + 5 =$ _______

2 $11 - 4 + 5 =$ _______ **5** $15 - 5 + 6 =$ _______

3 $3 + 8 - 4 =$ _______ **6** $12 + 4 - 1 =$ _______

Write as multiplication and solve.

7 $3 + 3 + 3 + 3 =$ _______________ = _______

8 $5 + 5 + 5 + 5 + 5 =$ _______________ = _______

9 $7 + 7 + 7 =$ _______________ = _______

10 $8 + 8 + 8 + 8 + 8 + 8 =$ _______________ = _______

11 $5 + 5 =$ _______________ = _______

12 $4 + 4 + 4 + 4 =$ _______________ = _______

13 $3 + 3 + 3 + 3 + 3 + 3 =$ _______________ = _______

14 $10 + 10 + 10 + 10 + 10 =$ _______________ = _______

15 $9 + 9 + 9 + 9 + 9 + 9 =$ _______________ = _______

▶ Fill in the graph to show how many you did correctly in one minute.

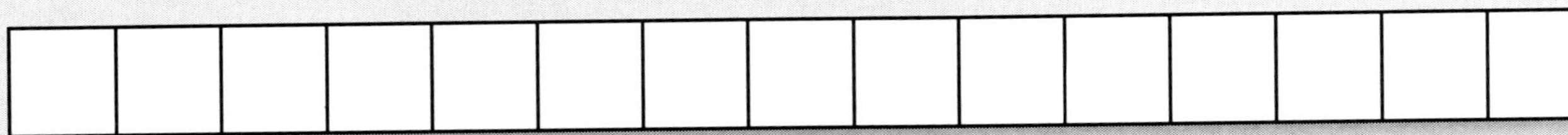

| 1 | 2 | 3 | 4 | 5 | 6 | 7 | 8 | 9 | 10 | 11 | 12 | 13 | 14 | 15 |

My goal for tomorrow is: _______
(Write in the number you want to get correct tomorrow.)

Arrays

Write two multiplication facts for each array.

1 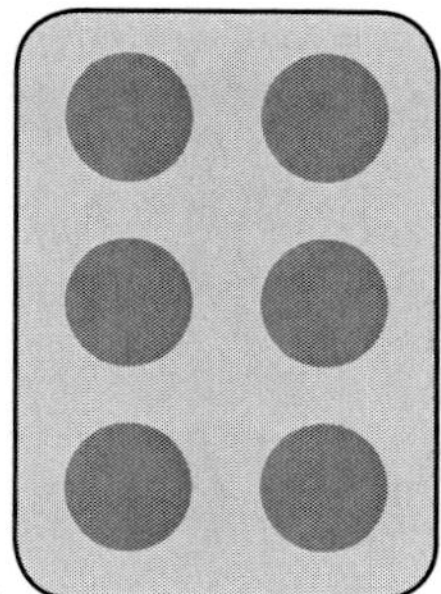

$3 \times 2 = \boxed{}$

$2 \times 3 = \boxed{}$

2 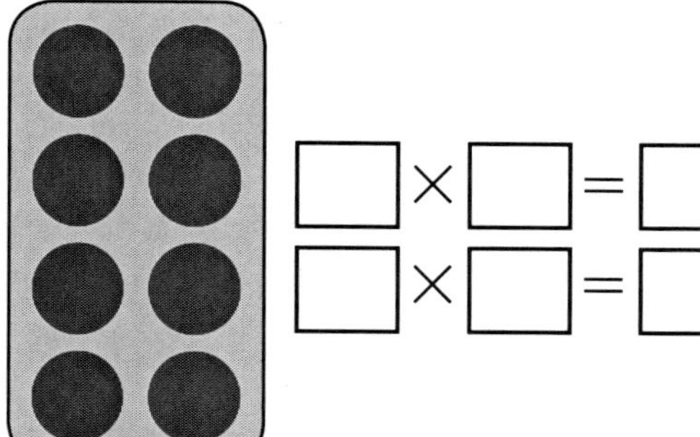

$\boxed{} \times \boxed{} = \boxed{}$

$\boxed{} \times \boxed{} = \boxed{}$

3 

$\boxed{} \times \boxed{} = \boxed{}$

$\boxed{} \times \boxed{} = \boxed{}$

4 

$\boxed{} \times \boxed{} = \boxed{}$

$\boxed{} \times \boxed{} = \boxed{}$

5 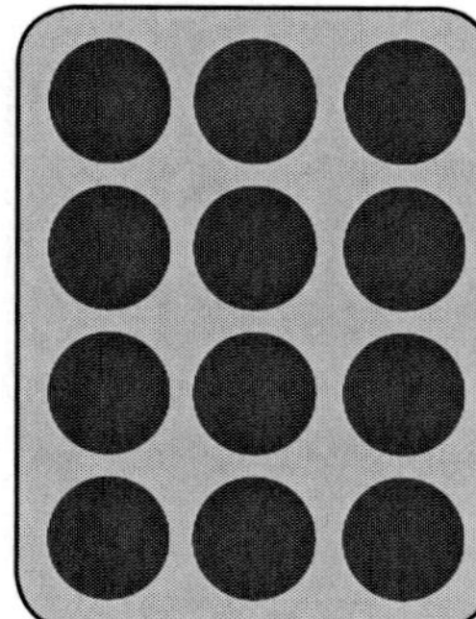

$\boxed{} \times \boxed{} = \boxed{}$

$\boxed{} \times \boxed{} = \boxed{}$

6 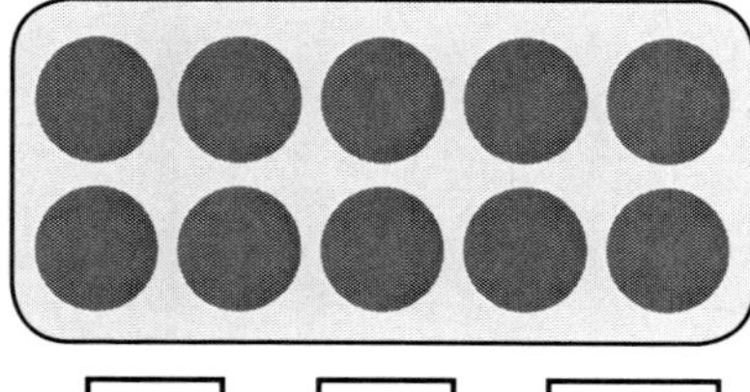

$\boxed{} \times \boxed{} = \boxed{}$

$\boxed{} \times \boxed{} = \boxed{}$

Draw a diagram

Use 24 counters. How many different arrays can you make? 

Draw them on grid paper. Write 2 multiplications facts for each.

Centimeter Grid

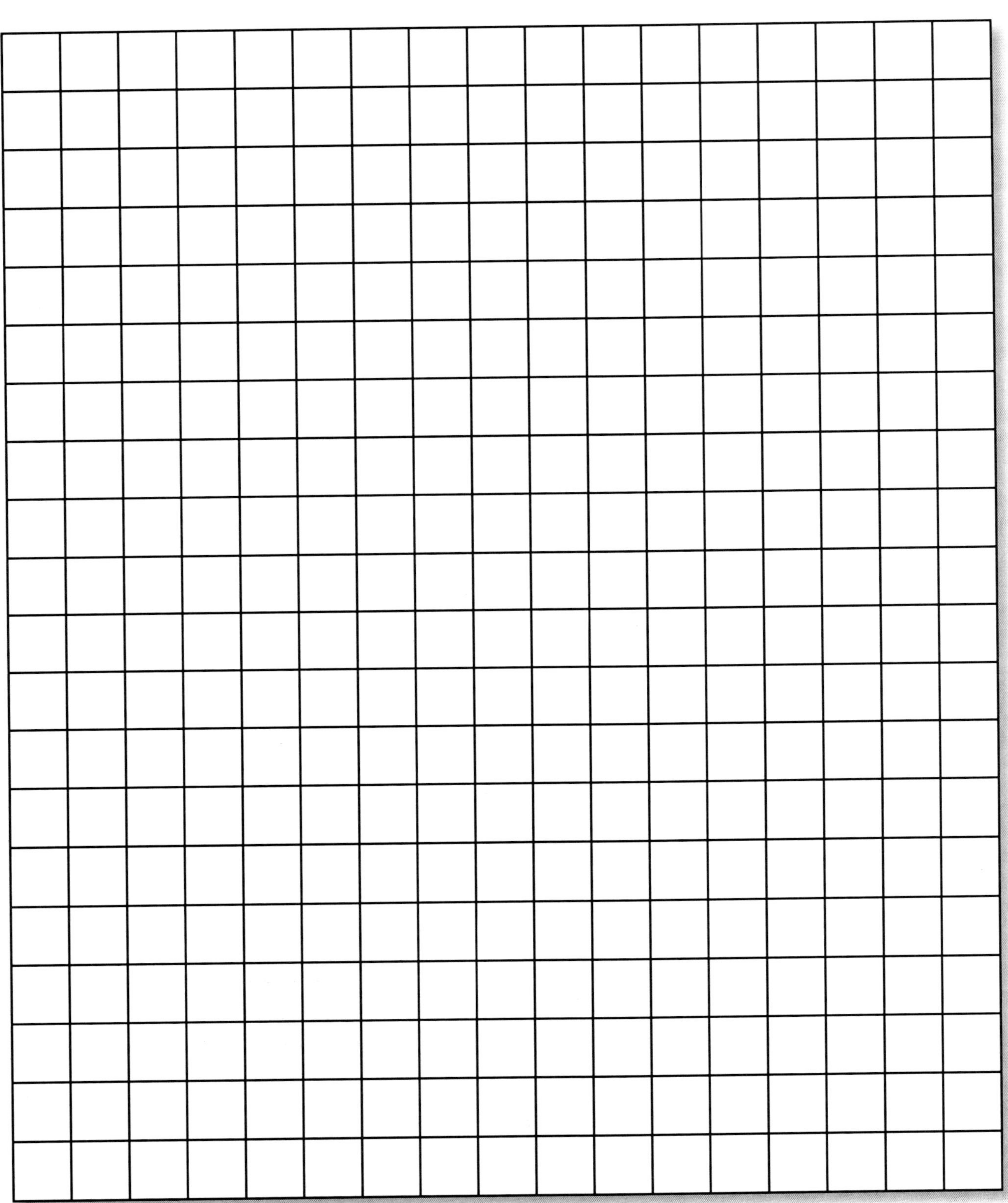

Model Multiplication

1 Complete the chart.

example 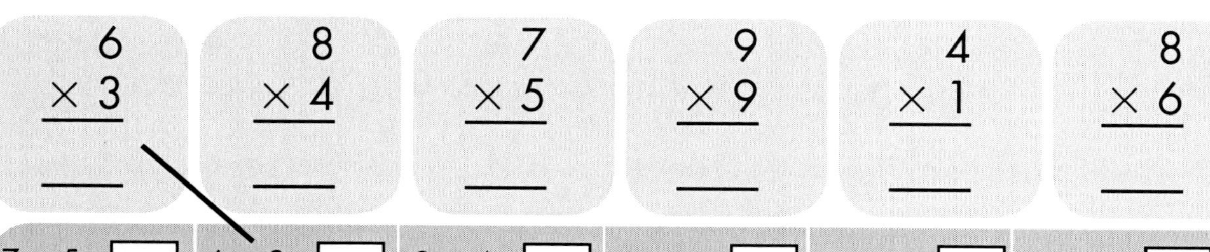	4 groups of 6	6 $\times$ 4	6 × 4	24
a	8 groups of 4			
b		6 $\times$ 6		
c				21

2 Write a number sentence and the product.

a 8 cars. 4 people in each car.
How many people? ☐ × ☐ = ☐

b 6 cases each holding 8 pencils.
How many pencils? ☐ × ☐ = ☐

3 Write the answers and match.

$$6 \times 3 \qquad 8 \times 4 \qquad 7 \times 5 \qquad 9 \times 9 \qquad 4 \times 1 \qquad 8 \times 6$$

7 × 5 = ☐   6 × 3 = ☐   8 × 4 = ☐   8 × 6 = ☐   9 × 9 = ☐   4 × 1 = ☐

7 × 9 = ☐   4 × 0 = ☐   10 × 3 = ☐   9 × 5 = ☐   6 × 2 = ☐   4 × 4 = ☐

$$4 \times 0 \qquad 10 \times 3 \qquad 7 \times 9 \qquad 6 \times 2 \qquad 4 \times 4 \qquad 9 \times 5$$

Name ___________________________________

Multiply.

1	$2 \times 4 =$ _______	**9**	$5 \times 4 =$ _______
2	$3 \times 5 =$ _______	**10**	$7 \times 5 =$ _______
3	$4 \times 10 =$ _______	**11**	$5 \times 10 =$ _______
4	$7 \times 2 =$ _______	**12**	$5 \times 5 =$ _______
5	$2 \times 5 =$ _______	**13**	$9 \times 5 =$ _______
6	$2 \times 8 =$ _______	**14**	$5 \times 6 =$ _______
7	$10 \times 1 =$ _______	**15**	$8 \times 5 =$ _______
8	$6 \times 2 =$ _______		

▶ Fill in the graph to show how many you did correctly in one minute.

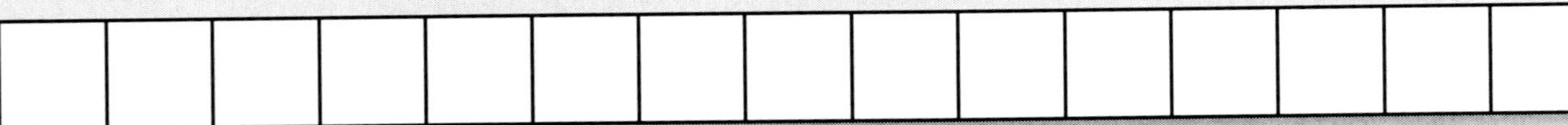

1	2	3	4	5	6	7	8	9	10	11	12	13	14	15

My goal for tomorrow is:______
(Write in the number you want to get correct tomorrow.)

Multiplication Facts

Multiply by 0.

You know that $4 \times 0 = 0$. You also know that $0 \times 7 = 0$.
Write a sentence about multiplying by 0. Use the words <u>factor</u>
and <u>product</u> in your fact.

____

____

____

Multiply by 1.

You know that $4 \times 1 = 4$. You also know that $1 \times 7 = 7$.
Write a fact about multiplying by 1. Use the words <u>factor</u> and
<u>product</u> in your fact.

____

____

____

Order.

You know that $4 \times 3 = 12$. You also know that $3 \times 4 = 12$.
Write a fact about order in multiplication. Use the words <u>factor</u>
and <u>product</u> in your fact.

____

____

____

Name _______________________________

Multiply.

1 $4 \times 4 =$ _______   **9** $0 \times 9 =$ _______

2 $0 \times 6 =$ _______   **10** $6 \times 0 =$ _______

3 $6 \times 1 =$ _______   **11** $6 \times 8 =$ _______

4 $4 \times 7 =$ _______   **12** $9 \times 7 =$ _______

5 $1 \times 9 =$ _______   **13** $3 \times 0 =$ _______

6 $4 \times 9 =$ _______   **14** $9 \times 6 =$ _______

7 $9 \times 8 =$ _______   **15** $16 \times 0 =$ _______

8 $4 \times 8 =$ _______

▶ Fill in the graph to show how many you did correctly in one minute.

1	2	3	4	5	6	7	8	9	10	11	12	13	14	15

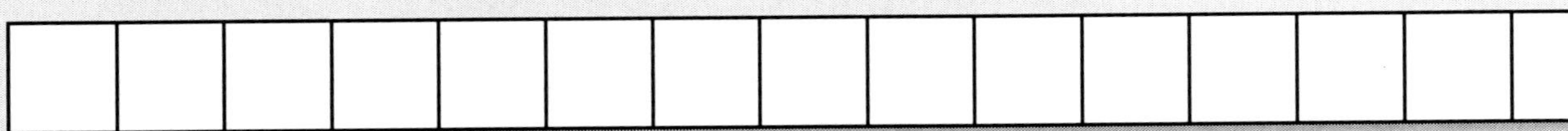

My goal for tomorrow is:______
(Write in the number you want to get correct tomorrow.)

Times Table

×	0	1	2	3	4	5	6	7	8	9	10
0											
1											
2											
3											
4											
5											
6											
7											
8											
9											
10											

WEEK THREE

Name _______________________________

Multiply.

1	$3 \times 7 =$ _______	**9**	$6 \times 9 =$ _______
2	$9 \times 9 =$ _______	**10**	$7 \times 6 =$ _______
3	$8 \times 6 =$ _______	**11**	$9 \times 8 =$ _______
4	$5 \times 0 =$ _______	**12**	$4 \times 8 =$ _______
5	$3 \times 8 =$ _______	**13**	$6 \times 6 =$ _______
6	$8 \times 10 =$ _______	**14**	$8 \times 5 =$ _______
7	$4 \times 6 =$ _______	**15**	$1 \times 7 =$ _______
8	$1 \times 9 =$ _______		

▶ Fill in the graph to show how many you did correctly in one minute.

1	2	3	4	5	6	7	8	9	10	11	12	13	14	15

Product Patterns

1 The table for 1 is done for you.

   a Write in the table for 4. Look for a pattern.

   b Write in the table for 3. Look for a pattern.

   c Write in the table for 7. Look for a pattern.

   d Complete the rest of the table. Shade all the doubles (like 5×5).

×	0	1	2	3	4	5	6	7	8	9	10
0		0									
1	0	1	2	3	4	5	6	7	8	9	10
2		2									
3		3									
4		4									
5		5									
6		6									
7		7									
8		8									
9		9									
10		10									

Name _______________________

Date _______________________

1 a How many groups? _____

 b How many pumpkins in each group? _____

 c How many pumpkins altogether? _____

 d ____ + ____ + ____ + ____ + ____ + ____ = ____

 e ____ × ____ = ____

2 Write the multiplication facts for the array.

 _______________________

3 Multiply.

 a $6 \times 0 =$ _____   **d** $0 \times 8 =$ _____   **g** $7 \times 9 =$ _____

 b $1 \times 9 =$ _____   **e** $5 \times 6 =$ _____   **h** $4 \times 4 =$ _____

 c $2 \times 1 =$ _____   **f** $3 \times 4 =$ _____

4 Count backwards in:

 a 6 from 36 ____ ____ ____ ____ ____

 b 8s from 40 ____ ____ ____ ____ ____

5 Julie is making 5 necklaces. There are 8 large beads on each. how many large beads will Julie need?

 ○ **a** 13   ○ **b** 35   ○ **c** 40

Name _______________________________

Date _______________________________

6 Write the numbers:

    a three hundred eight _____   **b** four hundred fifty-seven _____

7 Write in order. Start with the least number.

    390   309   399   319   380   331

    _____   _____   _____   _____   _____   _____

8 Write the number.

a    **b** 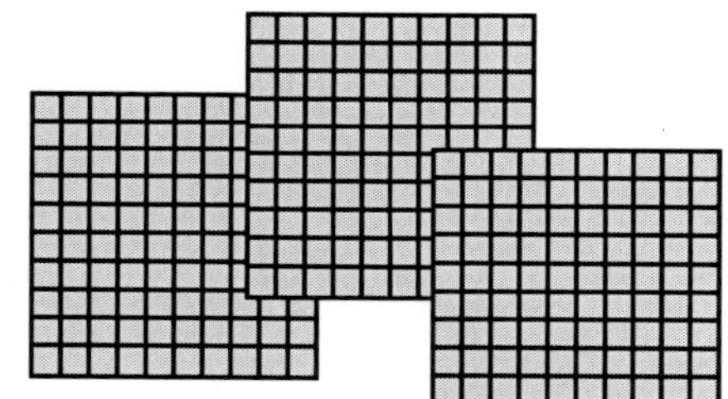

9 Find the total.

    a $34 + 26 =$ _____   **c** $176 + 38 =$ _____

    b $43 - 17 =$ _____   **d** $342 - 204 =$ _____

10 Sal jumped 44 inches and Sue jumped 66 inches.

    Write the difference in inches. [ ]

11 Which of the following is close to 100?

    ○ **a** $41 + 58$ ○ **b** $27 + 68$ ○ **c** $43 + 64$

WEEK **THREE**

Name ____

Solve.

1 $6 + 9 + 5 =$ _______

2 $0 \times 9 =$ _______

3 $13 + 9 - 11 =$ _______

4 $17 - 10 + 6 =$ _______

5 $7 \times 6 =$ _______

6 $21 - 6 - 11 =$ _______

7 $19 - 3 - 8 =$ _______

8 $17 + 13 =$ _______

9 $8 + 7 + 6 =$ _______

10 $9 \times 1 =$ _______

11 $17 + 2 - 8 =$ _______

12 $8 \times 8 =$ _______

13 $10 \times 10 =$ _______

14 $14 + 3 + 7 =$ _______

15 $23 - 15 - 7 =$ _______

▶ Fill in the graph to show how many you did correctly in one minute.

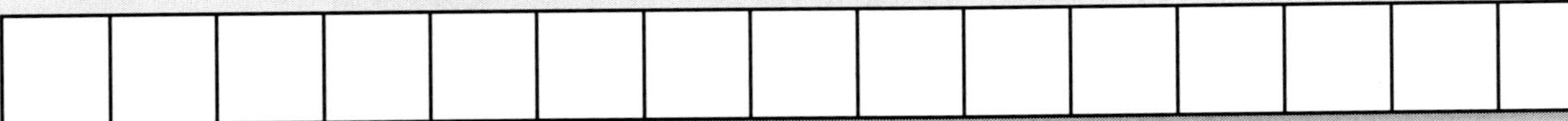

1	2	3	4	5	6	7	8	9	10	11	12	13	14	15

My goal for tomorrow is:______

(Write in the number you want to get correct tomorrow.)

Divide in Threes

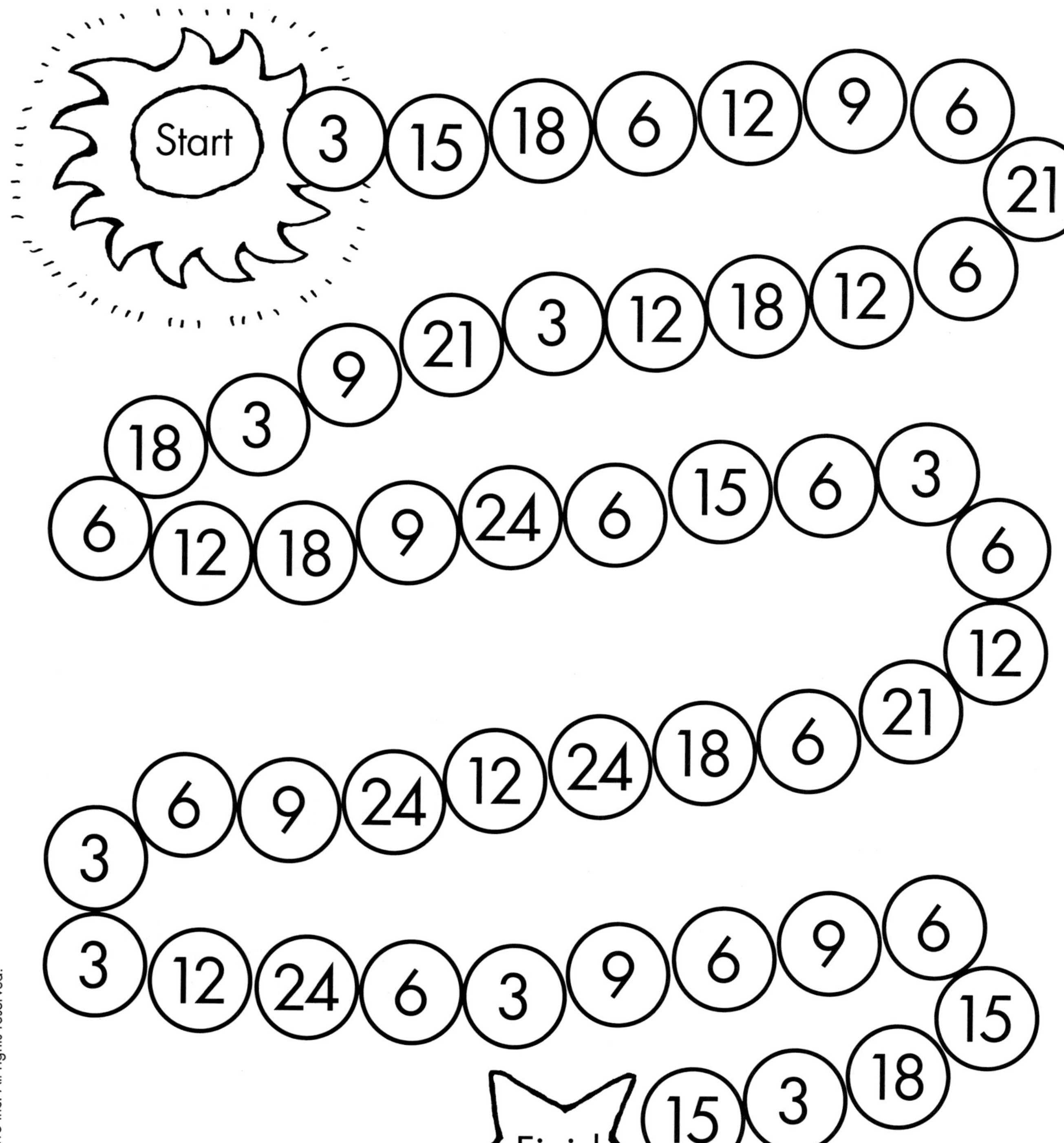

Prices, Yesterday and Today

You will work with a partner to compare prices from 50 years ago.

Part 1
- Look at the items listed on **Prices, Then and Now BLM 25**.

Part 2
- Look at how the prices have changed! Finding unit prices will show just how great the changes have been. Divide to figure out unit prices. A unit price is the cost of ONE item that comes in a pack of several. For instance, if a 3-pack of T-shirts costs $3, one T-shirt costs $1.
- Figure out how much more expensive each item is today than it was then. You can estimate, use a calculator, divide with models, use repeated subtraction, or any other method that works for you. Write your answers in the table.

Part 3
- Use **Shopping List BLM 27** to make up two family shopping lists: one based on 1955 prices, and one based on 2005 prices. You can spend up to $30. Shop carefully! What amount of today's money compares with $30 in 1955? On Friday, you will post the shopping lists.

Prices, Then and Now

Here are some prices for items you may use.

Foods	1955 Price	2005 Price	1955 Unit Price	2005 Unit Price	How many times more is today's cost?
1 gallon milk (= 4 quarts)	$1.00	$3.00	.25 per quart	.75 per quart	3 times more
1 loaf bread (= 10 ounces)	20¢	$1.20			
1 chicken (= 3 pounds)	75¢	$3.00			
1 dozen eggs (= 12 eggs)	60¢	$1.20			
1 tin coffee (= 8 ounces)	48¢	$1.44			
1 bag potatoes (= 5 pounds)	30¢	$2.10			
1 can tuna (= 6 ounces)	24¢	72¢			
2-pack tomatoes	32¢	96¢			
1 pound apples (= 4 apples)	20¢	80¢			
1 bag oranges (= 3 oranges)	33¢	$1.32			
4-pack of yogurt	88¢	$2.64			
3-pack juice boxes	33¢	99¢			
5-pack string cheese	$1.00	$2.00			
8 hot dogs	$1.60	$3.20			
8 hot dog buns	72¢	$1.44			
5-pack ice pops	$1.00	$3.00			

Other Items	1955 Price	2005 Price	1955 Unit Price	2005 Unit Price	How many times more is today's cost?
10 stamps	30¢	$3.70			
2 toothbrushes	60¢	$2.40			
2-pack of soap	30¢	$1.20			
5-pack of kid's movie tickets	$1.75				
weekly newspaper (= 7 days)	35¢	$3.85			
10-pack of pencils	60¢	$1.80			
8-pack of crayons	72¢	$1.44			

Name _______________________________

How many in each equal group?

1 24 in 6 groups _______   **9** 42 in 6 groups _______

2 36 in 4 groups _______   **10** 35 in 5 groups _______

3 18 in 3 groups _______   **11** 54 in 6 groups _______

4 20 in 5 groups _______   **12** 18 in 6 groups _______

5 36 in 6 groups _______   **13** 16 in 4 groups _______

6 24 in 8 groups _______   **14** 27 in 9 groups _______

7 21 in 3 groups _______   **15** 40 in 5 groups _______

8 54 in 9 groups _______

▶ Fill in the graph to show how many you did correctly in one minute.

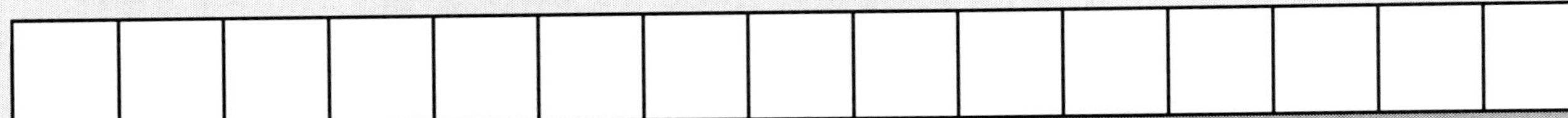

| 1 | 2 | 3 | 4 | 5 | 6 | 7 | 8 | 9 | 10 | 11 | 12 | 13 | 14 | 15 |

My goal for tomorrow is:_______

(Write in the number you want to get correct tomorrow.)

Egg Carton Division

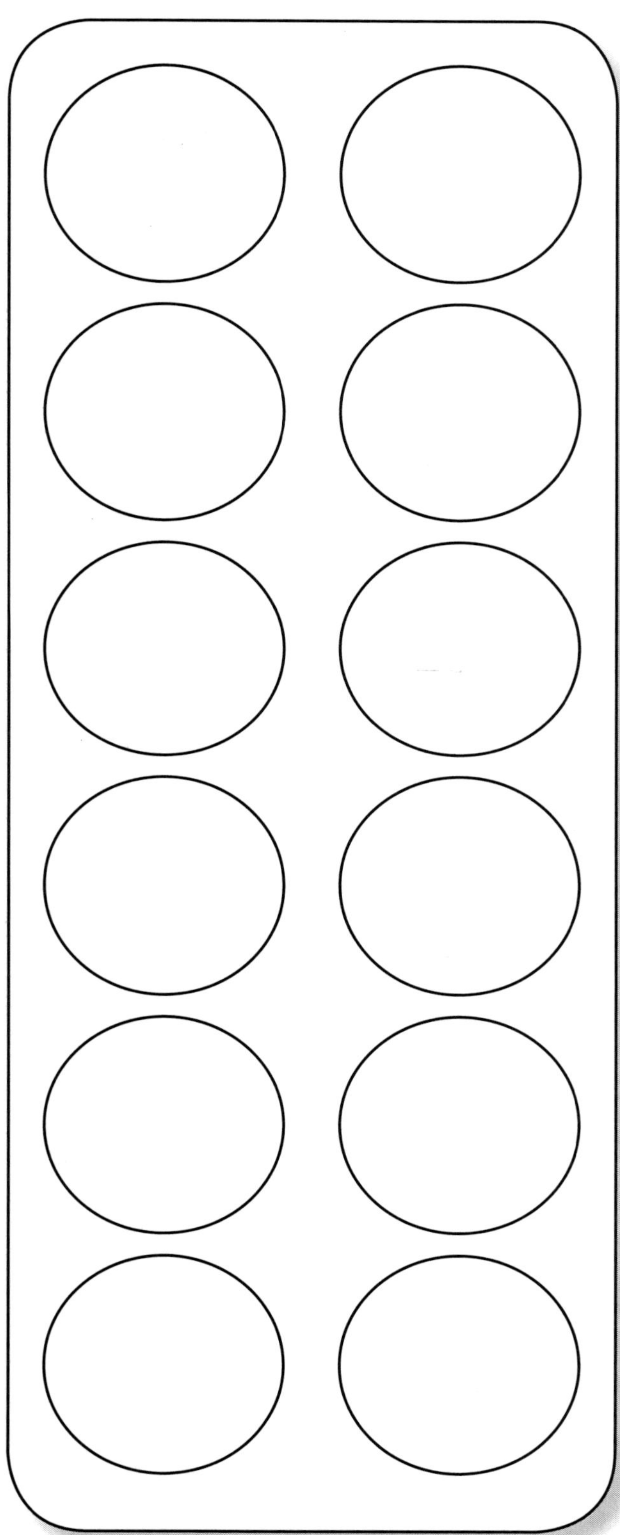

Name ____

Write three more facts for each.

$7 \times 8 = 56$ **1** _________   **2** _________   **3** _________

$9 \times 4 = 36$ **4** _________   **5** _________   **6** _________

$6 \times 9 = 54$ **7** _________   **8** _________   **9** _________

$48 \div 6 = 8$ **10** _________   **11** _________   **12** _________

$63 \div 7 = 9$ **13** _________   **14** _________   **15** _________

▶ Fill in the graph to show how many you did correctly in one minute.

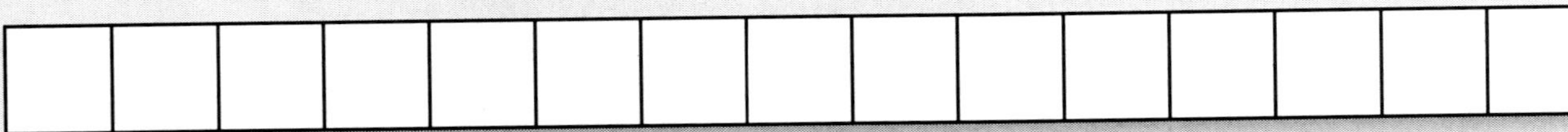

1	2	3	4	5	6	7	8	9	10	11	12	13	14	15

My goal for tomorrow is: ______

(Write in the number you want to get correct tomorrow.)

Shopping List

Record what you could buy. Do one list for 1955 and another for now. You may spend up to $30. Think about the needs of a family of 3 people for a week.

How Many?	Item	Price for Each	Total Price
		TOTAL	

WEEK FOUR

Sharing Dogs

1   These dogs all need good homes. How many dogs are there? _________

2   How many dogs would each person get if they were fairly shared by:

   a 4 people? _________   **b** 3 people? _________

   c 12 people? _________   **d** 24 people? _________

3   Tom took half the dogs. How many did he take? _________

4   Eve found 5 families to take some dogs.

   How many will each family take? _________

   How many dogs will still need homes? _________

Name ______________________________________

Solve.

1 $6 \times 6 =$ _________ **9** $6 \times 8 =$ _________

2 $45 \div 5 =$ _________ **10** $7 \div 7 =$ _________

3 $8 \times 9 =$ _________ **11** $9 \times 4 =$ _________

4 $56 \div 7 =$ _________ **12** $54 \div 6 =$ _________

5 $6 \times 7 =$ _________ **13** $9 \times 3 =$ _________

6 $72 \div 9 =$ _________ **14** $24 \div 8 =$ _________

7 $0 \times 6 =$ _________ **15** $7 \times 7 =$ _________

8 $32 \div 4 =$ _________

▶ Fill in the graph to show how many you did correctly in one minute.

1	2	3	4	5	6	7	8	9	10	11	12	13	14	15

My goal for tomorrow is: ______

(Write in the number you want to get correct tomorrow.)

Hundred Grid

1	2	3	4	5	6	7	8	9	10
11	12	13	14	15	16	17	18	19	20
21	22	23	24	25	26	27	28	29	30
31	32	33	34	35	36	37	38	39	40
41	42	43	44	45	46	47	48	49	50
51	52	53	54	55	56	57	58	59	60
61	62	63	64	65	66	67	68	69	70
71	72	73	74	75	76	77	78	79	80
81	82	83	84	85	86	87	88	89	90
91	92	93	94	95	96	97	98	99	100

Name ___________________________________

Divide.

1	$48 \div 8 =$ _______	**9**	$32 \div 8 =$ _______
2	$80 \div 8 =$ _______	**10**	$24 \div 8 =$ _______
3	$42 \div 7 =$ _______	**11**	$70 \div 7 =$ _______
4	$56 \div 7 =$ _______	**12**	$56 \div 8 =$ _______
5	$49 \div 7 =$ _______	**13**	$21 \div 7 =$ _______
6	$28 \div 7 =$ _______	**14**	$40 \div 8 =$ _______
7	$64 \div 8 =$ _______	**15**	$35 \div 7 =$ _______
8	$63 \div 7 =$ _______		

▶ Fill in the graph to show how many you did correctly in one minute.

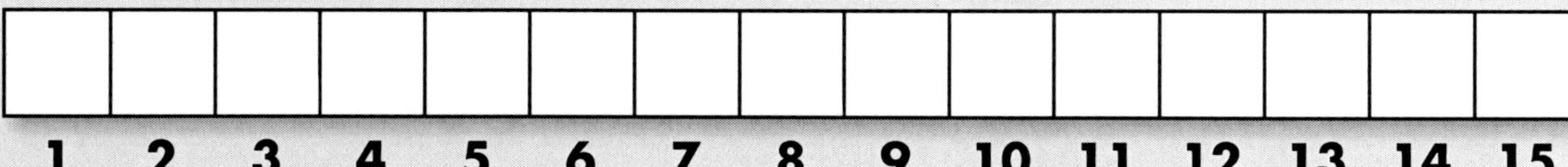

Division Dots

1 4 groups
⑥⟌ ⊡ ⊡ ⊡ ⊡ | 24 |

24 ÷ 6

2 _____ groups
◯⟌ ☐

3 _____ groups
◯⟌ ☐

4 _____ groups
◯⟌ ☐

5 _____ groups
◯⟌ ☐

6 _____ groups
◯⟌ ☐

Name _______________________________

Date _______________________________

1 How many in each group? Use these stars to help.

   a 4 equal groups _______

   b 6 equal groups _______

   c 2 equal groups _______

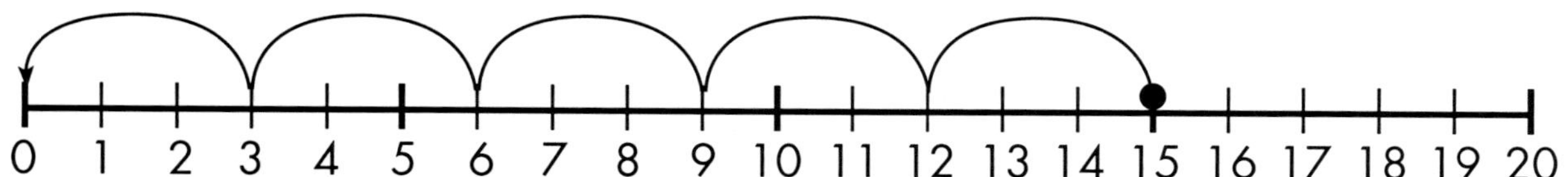

2 How many 3s in 15? _______

There are _______ 3s in 15. $15 \div 3 =$ _______

3 Complete.

   a $6 \times 9 =$ _______   **b** $7 \times 6 =$ _______

      $54 \div 6 =$ _______ $42 \div 7 =$ _______

      $54 \div 9 =$ _______ $42 \div 6 =$ _______

4 Complete.

   a $8\overline{)64} =$ _______   **b** $9\overline{)63} =$ _______   **c** $5\overline{)45} =$ _______

5 Use these keys to help.

   a $25 \div 4 =$ _______ remainder _______

   b $16 \div 3 =$ _______ remainder _______

   c $20 \div 6 =$ _______ remainder _______

   d $50 \div 8 =$ _______ remainder _______

6 Which is the correct answer to $3\overline{)26}$?

   ◯ **a** 6 R3   ◯ **b** 7 R4   ◯ **c** 8 R2

Name ________________________________

Solve.

1 $2 \times 8 =$ _____

2 $5 \times 7 =$ _____

3 $4 \times 6 =$ _____

4 $9 \times 10 =$ _____

5 $8 \times 4 =$ _____

6 $4 \times 0 =$ _____

7 $213 + 100 =$ _____

8 $649 - 100 =$ _____

9 $361 - 10 =$ _____

10 $20 - 9 =$ _____

11 $16 - 7 =$ _____

12 $8 + 5 =$ _____

13 $4 + 9 =$ _____

14 $11 + 8 =$ _____

15 $37 + 20 =$ _____

▶ Fill in the graph to show how many you did correctly in one minute.

1	2	3	4	5	6	7	8	9	10	11	12	13	14	15

My goal for tomorrow is: _____

(Write in the number you want to get correct tomorrow.)

Fractional Parts

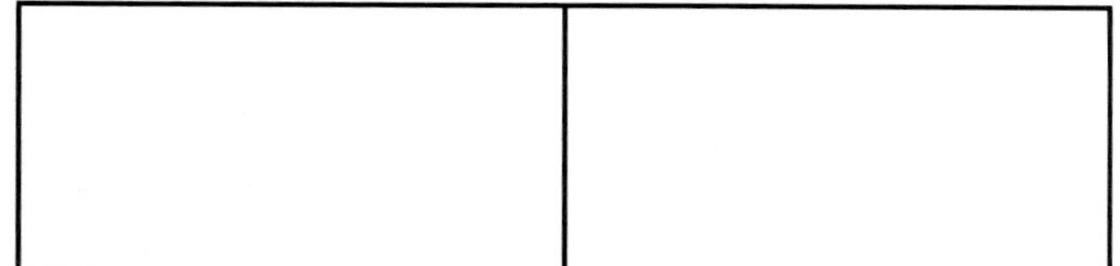

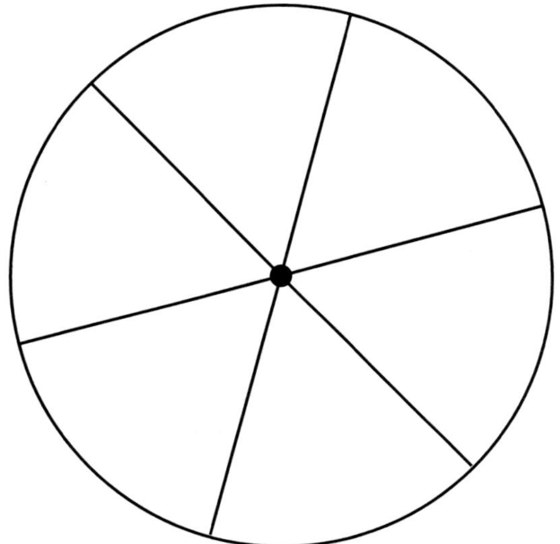

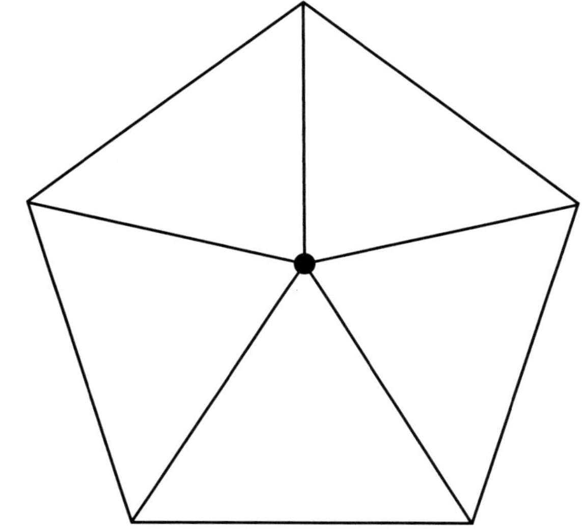

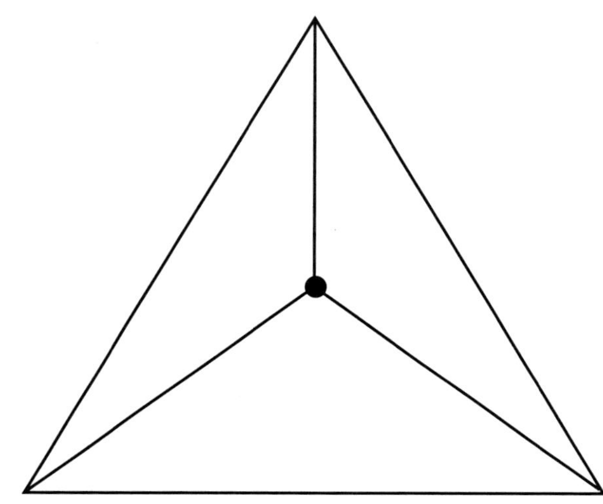

Mystery Math Day

Work with a partner to make up your own Math Number Puzzles to play on Friday.

Part 1

Fraction Math Machine

- Cut out shapes from **Fractional Parts BLM 31** and glue each on a card.
- Shade some parts of each shape. You decide how many.
- Make clue cards to match each shape card.

| $\frac{1}{2}$ | 1 out of 2 | $\frac{2}{3}$ | 2 out of 3 |

- Mix up the cards and store them.

Part 2

- Make up "Who Am I?" puzzles. Write a puzzle on the front of a card and the answer on the back. Try to write some puzzles about your class. Suppose 5 of 12 students wear glasses. Here is a puzzle you could write:

| I show part of a group. I tell something about eyes. What fraction am I? What group am I about? | $\frac{5}{12}$ of the students wear glasses |

(FRONT)

(BACK)

Part 3

- Put your puzzle, along with your classmates', in a grabbag. Take one out and solve it.

Name ___________________________

Solve.

1	$3 \times 9 =$ _____	**9**	$4 \times 8 =$ _____
2	$18 \div 2 =$ _____	**10**	$48 \div 6 =$ _____
3	$6 \times 7 =$ _____	**11**	$8 \times 8 =$ _____
4	$40 \div 8 =$ _____	**12**	$16 \div 4 =$ _____
5	$7 \times 9 =$ _____	**13**	$7 \times 7 =$ _____
6	$21 \div 3 =$ _____	**14**	$56 \div 7 =$ _____
7	$9 \times 9 =$ _____	**15**	$0 \times 4 =$ _____
8	$5 \div 5 =$ _____		

▶ Fill in the graph to show how many you did correctly in one minute.

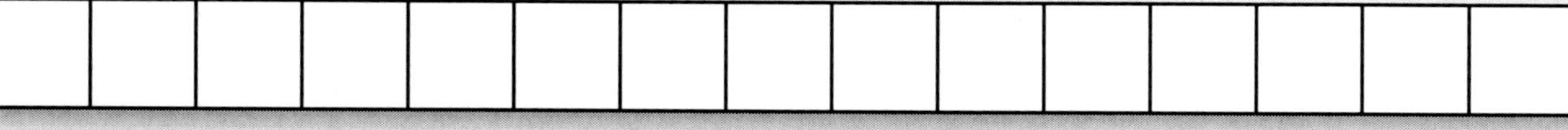

1	2	3	4	5	6	7	8	9	10	11	12	13	14	15

My goal for tomorrow is: _____

(Write in the number you want to get correct tomorrow.)

WEEK **FIVE**

Fraction Figures

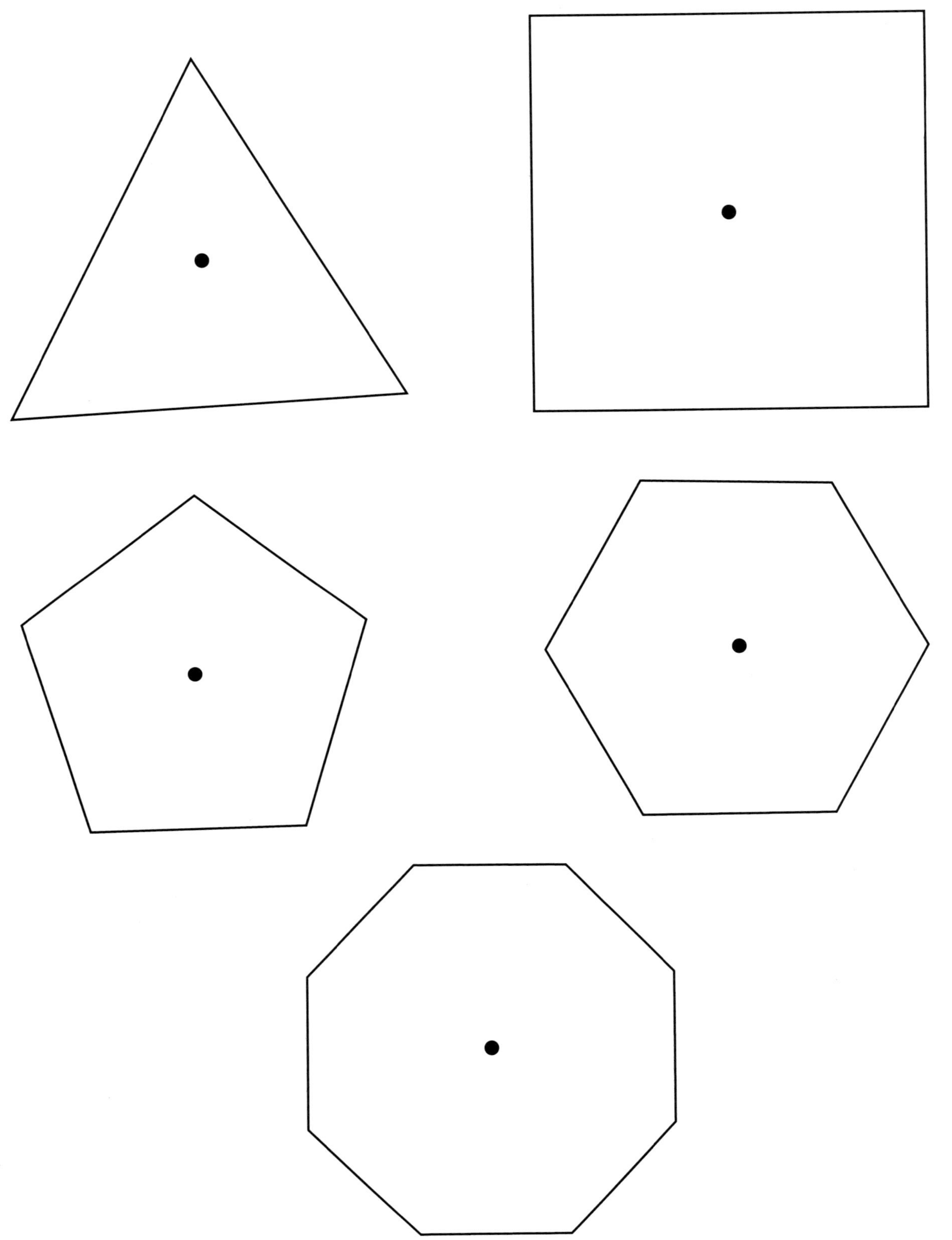

Name ________________________________

Solve.

1	$4 \times 2 =$ _____	**9**	$10 \div 5 =$ _____
2	$5 \times 3 =$ _____	**10**	$9 \div 3 =$ _____
3	$6 \times 5 =$ _____	**11**	$12 \div 2 =$ _____
4	$2 \times 8 =$ _____	**12**	$30 \div 5 =$ _____
5	$7 \times 3 =$ _____	**13**	$18 \div 2 =$ _____
6	$5 \times 1 =$ _____	**14**	$30 \div 3 =$ _____
7	$10 \times 2 =$ _____	**15**	$5 \times 5 =$ _____
8	$8 \div 2 =$ _____		

▶ Fill in the graph to show how many you did correctly in one minute.

1	2	3	4	5	6	7	8	9	10	11	12	13	14	15

My goal for tomorrow is: _____

(Write in the number you want to get correct tomorrow.)

WEEK **FIVE**

Even Number Cards

4	8
12	16
20	24
28	32
36	40

Name _________________________________

Look at the parts of the circles.

Circle the greater fraction.

1 $\frac{1}{2}$ $\frac{1}{5}$

2 $\frac{1}{4}$ $\frac{1}{2}$

3 $\frac{3}{4}$ $\frac{3}{8}$

4 $\frac{2}{8}$ $\frac{1}{10}$

5 $\frac{2}{5}$ $\frac{2}{10}$

6 $\frac{1}{4}$ $\frac{3}{8}$

7 $\frac{1}{2}$ $\frac{3}{5}$

8 $\frac{4}{5}$ $\frac{6}{10}$

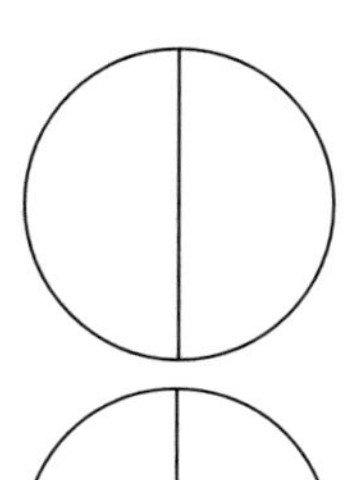
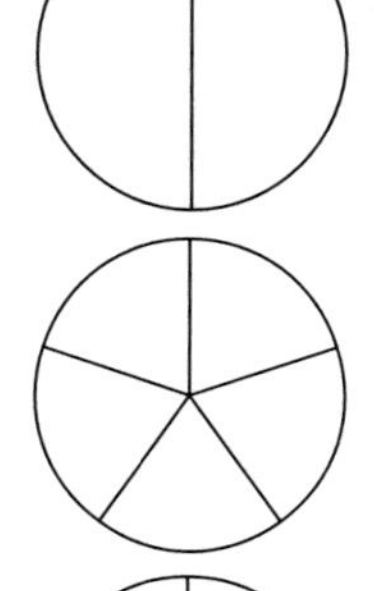
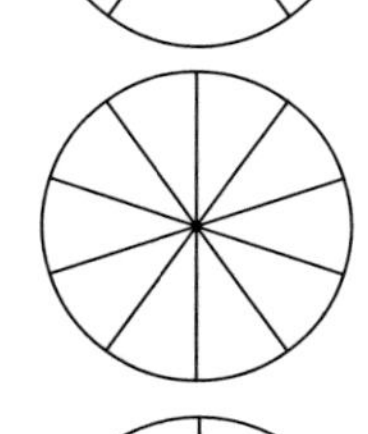
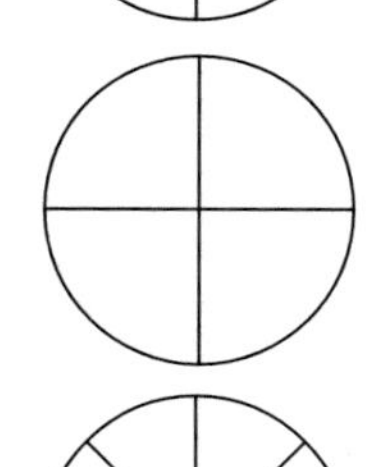
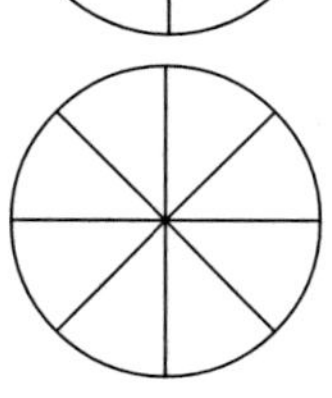

Use <, > or = .

9 $\frac{1}{2}$ _______ $\frac{1}{4}$

10 $\frac{1}{2}$ _______ $\frac{5}{10}$

11 $\frac{1}{5}$ _______ $\frac{5}{10}$

12 $\frac{3}{4}$ _______ $\frac{1}{2}$

13 $\frac{1}{4}$ _______ $\frac{1}{10}$

14 $\frac{2}{4}$ _______ $\frac{5}{10}$

15 $\frac{3}{5}$ _______ $\frac{4}{10}$

▶ Fill in the graph to show how many you did correctly in one minute.

| 1 | 2 | 3 | 4 | 5 | 6 | 7 | 8 | 9 | 10 | 11 | 12 | 13 | 14 | 15 |

My goal for tomorrow is: _______

(Write in the number you want to get correct tomorrow.)

WEEK **FIVE**

Fraction Strips

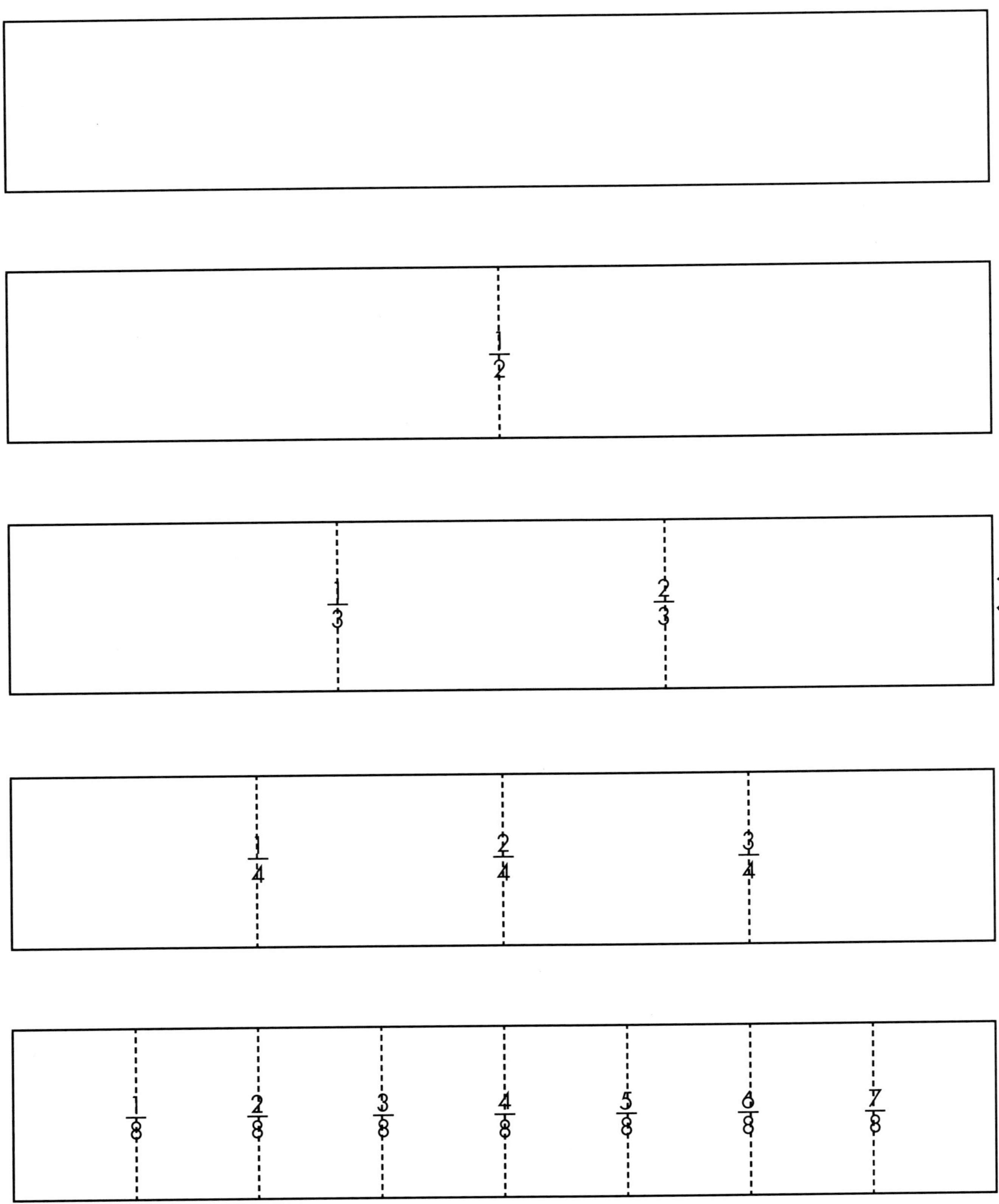

Estimating Fractions

What part is shaded? Circle the fraction.

1

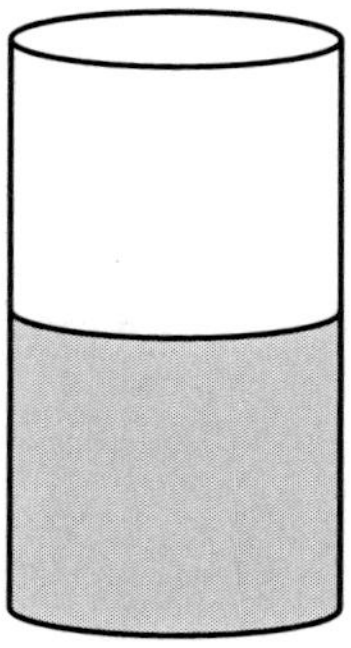

$\frac{1}{2}$ $\frac{3}{4}$

2

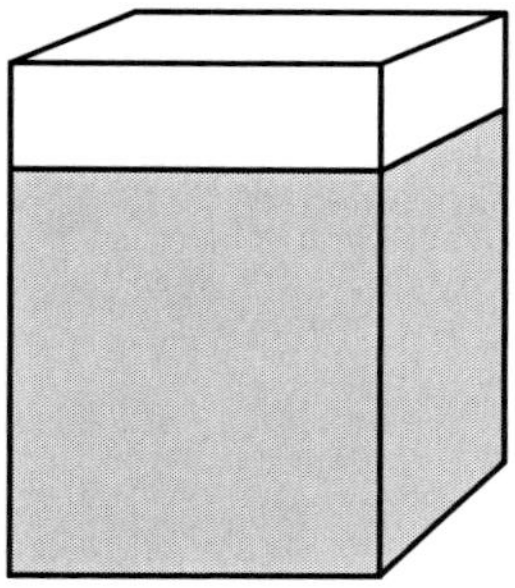

$\frac{1}{2}$ $\frac{3}{4}$

3

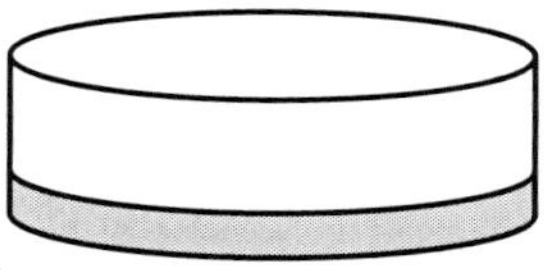

$\frac{1}{4}$ $\frac{1}{2}$

4

$\frac{1}{2}$ $\frac{2}{3}$

5

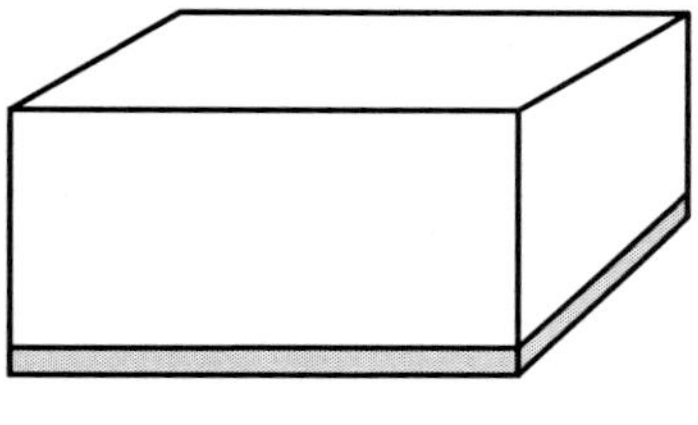

$\frac{1}{8}$ $\frac{1}{4}$ $\frac{1}{2}$

6

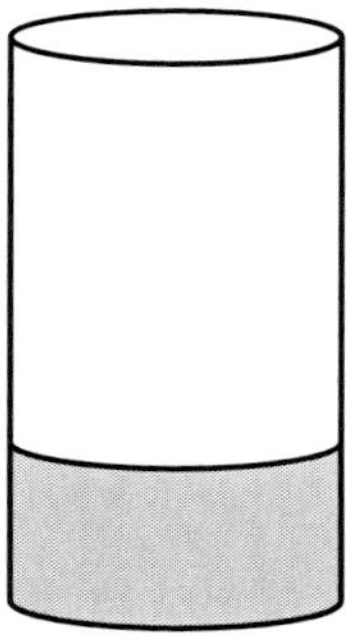

$\frac{1}{4}$ $\frac{1}{2}$

Shade each container.

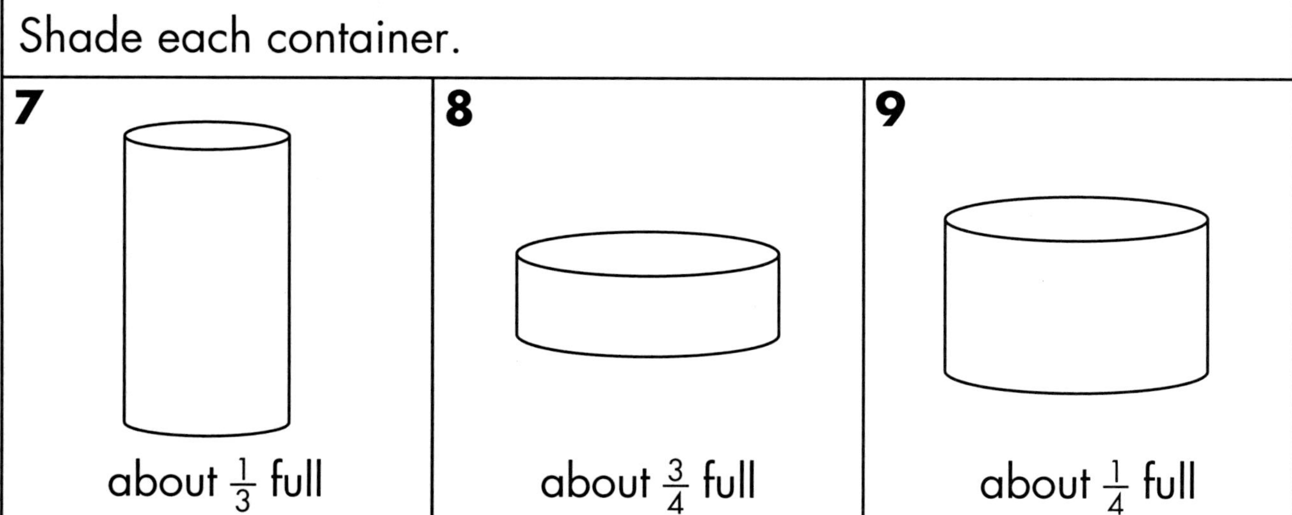

7

about $\frac{1}{3}$ full

8

about $\frac{3}{4}$ full

9

about $\frac{1}{4}$ full

WEEK **FIVE**

Name _______________________________

1 Shade half of A.
2 Shade one quarter of B.
3 Shade one quarter of C.
4 Shade half of D.
5 Shade one whole of E.
6 half of 20 = _____
7 quarter of 16 = _____
8 quarter of 28 = _____

Draw in lines to:
9 cut F in half.
10 cut G into quarters.
11 cut H in half.
12 cut I into quarters.
13 half of 50 = _____
14 quarter of 40 = _____
15 half of 24 = _____

A 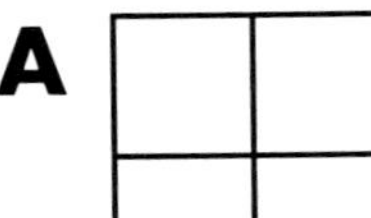 B 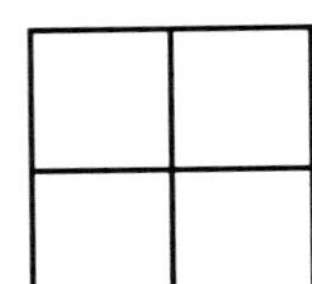

C 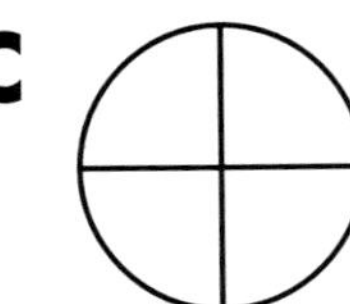 D 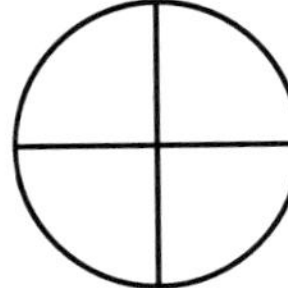

E 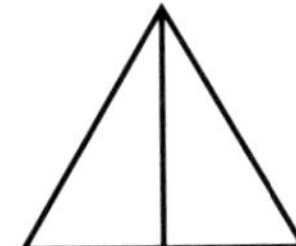 F 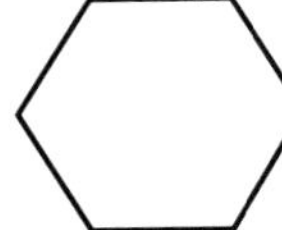

G 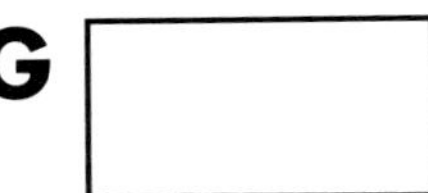 H 

I 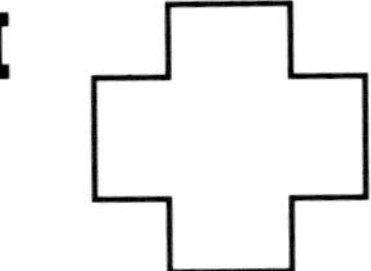

▶ Fill in the graph to show how many you did correctly in one minute.

1	2	3	4	5	6	7	8	9	10	11	12	13	14	15

Inch Ruler

Inches
1 2 3 4 5 6 7 8 9 10

WEEK **FIVE**

Name _______________________________

Date _______________________________

1 Circle objects which have $\frac{1}{2}$ shaded.

a **b** **c** **d** **e**

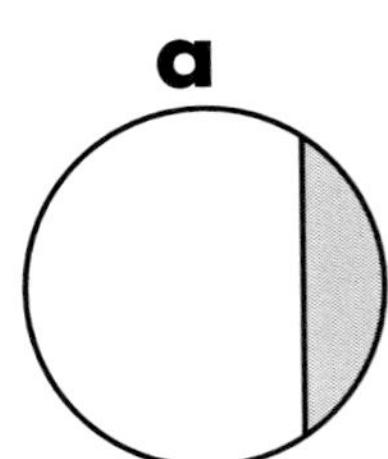 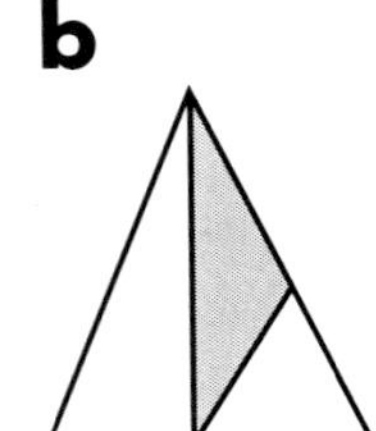 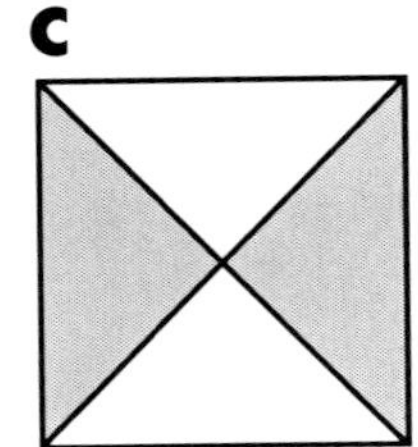 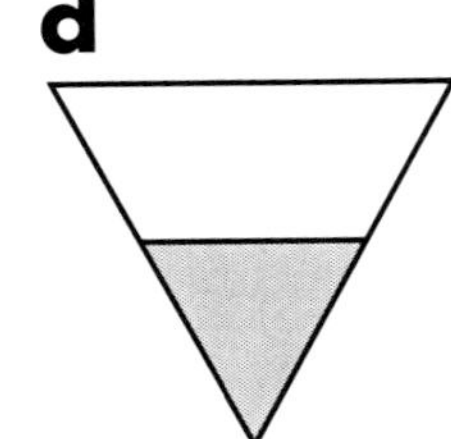 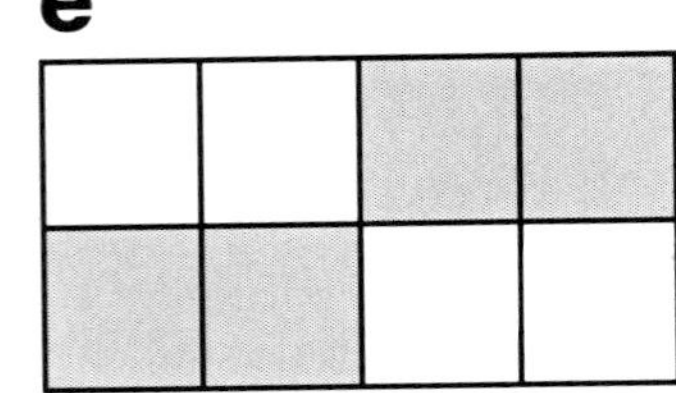

2 Circle half of each group.

3 How many in 1 whole?

a halves ____ **b** quarters ____ **c** fifths ____ **d** tenths ____

4 Joe has 12 oranges. How many make:

a $\frac{1}{2}$?____ **b** $\frac{2}{3}$?____ **c** $\frac{1}{3}$? ____ **d** $\frac{3}{4}$?____

5 A pen is longer than 3 inches but shorter than 4 inches. Which length could it be?

a $4\frac{1}{2}$ inches

b $3\frac{1}{4}$ inches

c $2\frac{3}{4}$ inches

Name ___________________________________

Write the number.

1 three hundred thirty-nine _______

2 seven hundred thirteen _______

3 two hundred nine _______

4 six hundred fifty _______

5 one thousand, two hundred fifty-six _______

6 seven thousand, one hundred ninety-nine _______

7 eight thousand, seven hundred nineteen _______

8 three thousand, three hundred thirty _______

Circle the least number.

9 320   302

10 989   997

11 2,692   2,962

12 4,190   4,910

13 8,223   8,322

14 7,051   5,703

15 3,999   2,399

▶ Fill in the graph to show how many you did correctly in one minute.

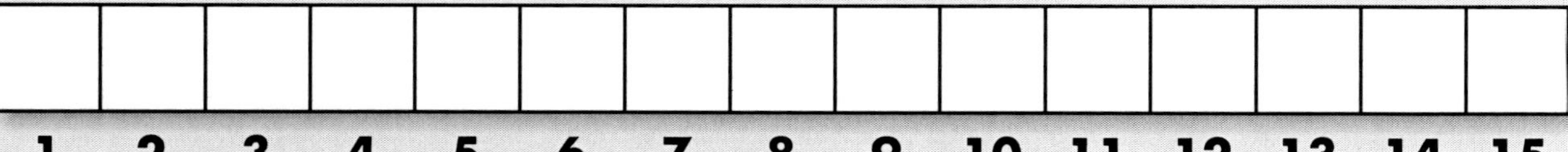

1	2	3	4	5	6	7	8	9	10	11	12	13	14	15

My goal for tomorrow is: _______

(Write in the number you want to get correct tomorrow.)

Decimal Party Plan

Pretend to give a Math Studio Decimal Party.
Think about refreshments, supplies, and games.

Part 1

• You are allowed to spend $5.00 per person. Count by 5s to figure out the total amount of money you will have to spend for your party.

Part 2

• Look through grocery ads to find the prices of items you need.

• Draw a chart like this and record the items and prices you found, including decimals.

Items	Price

Part 3

• Find your total. Did you spend too much? Decorate a menu listing your items from most expensive to least expensive.

Part 4

• Make up your own Decimal Game to play at your party.

Memory Math Game

0.1	$\frac{1}{10}$	**0.2**
$\frac{1}{2}$	**0.5**	$\frac{2}{10}$
0.4	$\frac{3}{4}$	**0.75**
$\frac{4}{10}$	**0.8**	$\frac{8}{10}$

Name ___________________________

Solve.

1 half of 16 = _____ **2** half of 12 = _____ **3** quarter of 8 = _____

Write the number.

4 six hundred fifty ___________

5 three hundred seven ___________

6 eight hundred six ___________

7 five less than forty-three ___________

8 4th number after 97 ___________

9 number between 199 and 201 ___________

10 42 = _____ + _____   **13** 273 = _____ + _____ + _____

11 80 = _____ + _____   **14** 918 = _____ + _____ + _____

12 115 = _____ + _____ + _____   **15** 605 = _____ + _____ + _____

▶ Fill in the graph to show how many you did correctly in one minute.

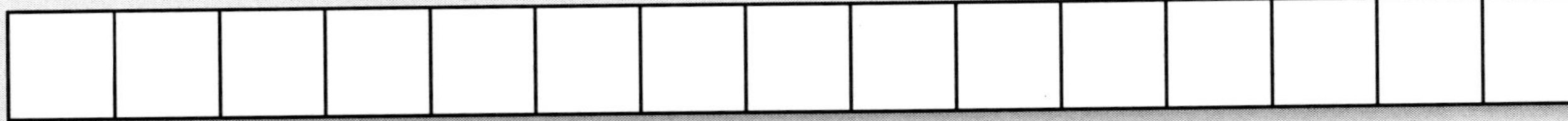

1	2	3	4	5	6	7	8	9	10	11	12	13	14	15

My goal for tomorrow is: _____

(Write in the number you want to get correct tomorrow.)

Decimal Grids

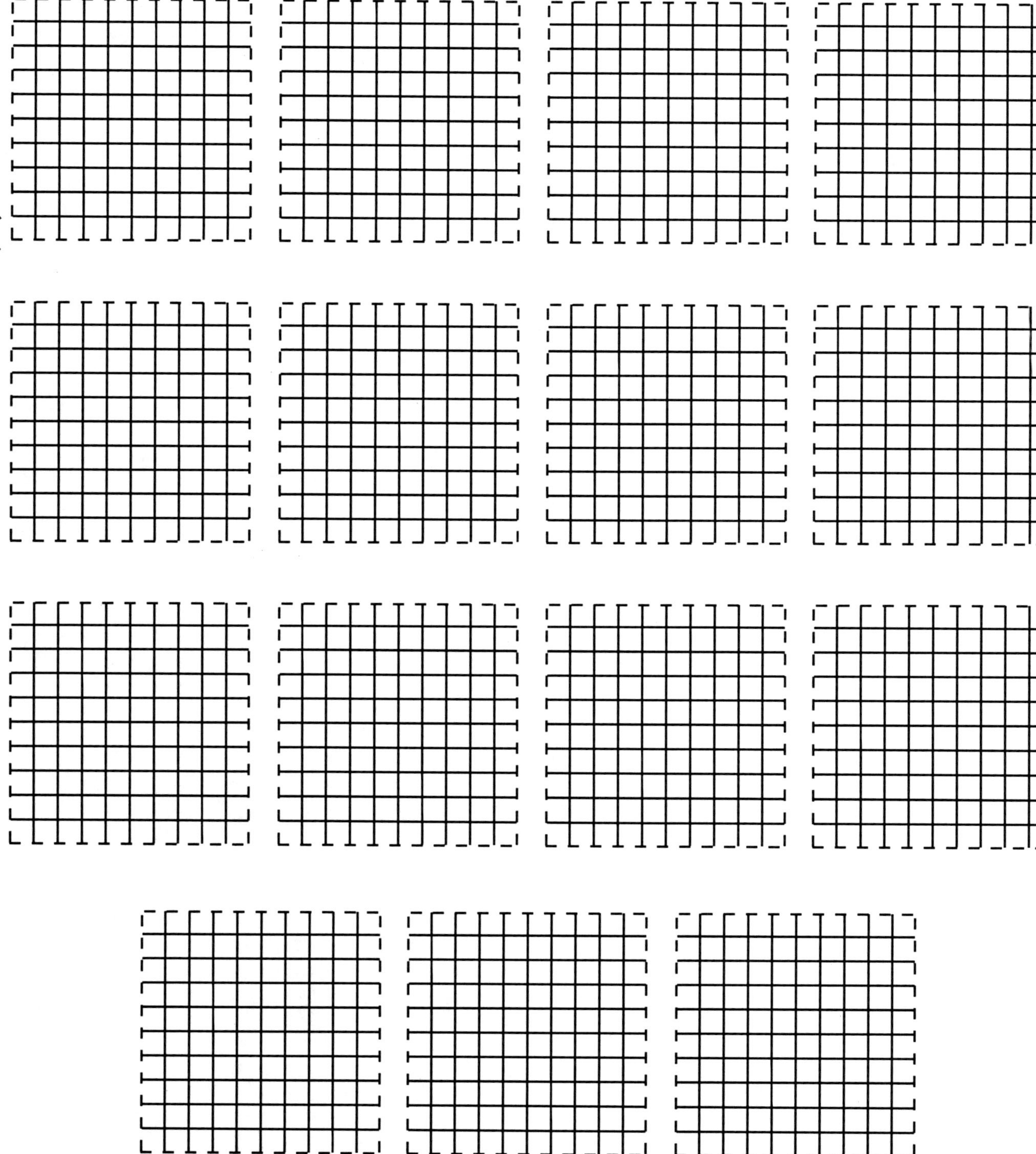

Name ______________________________

Match.

1	$\frac{25}{100}$	0.90
2	$\frac{50}{100}$	$\frac{1}{4}$
3	$\frac{90}{100}$	$\frac{100}{100}$
4	1	0.50
5	$\frac{7}{100}$	0.85
6	0.75	0.07
7	0.32	$\frac{3}{4}$
8	$\frac{85}{100}$	$\frac{32}{100}$

Use >, <, or =.

9 $\frac{1}{4}$ __________ $\frac{1}{2}$

10 0.25 __________ $\frac{1}{4}$

11 $\frac{1}{2}$ __________ $\frac{5}{10}$

12 $\frac{5}{10}$ __________ $\frac{1}{5}$

13 0.35 __________ $\frac{5}{100}$

14 $\frac{10}{10}$ __________ 1

15 $\frac{1}{5}$ __________ $\frac{1}{10}$

▶ Fill in the graph to show how many you did correctly in one minute.

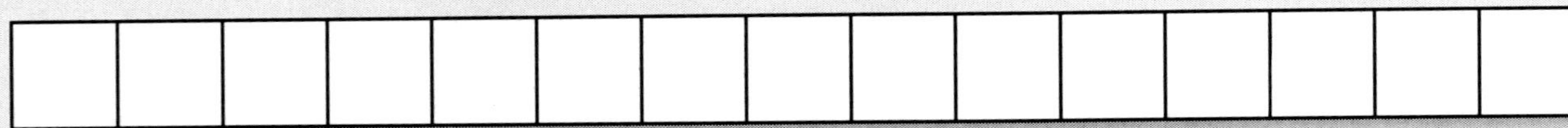

1	2	3	4	5	6	7	8	9	10	11	12	13	14	15

My goal for tomorrow is: ______

(Write in the number you want to get correct tomorrow.)

Making Half Grid

toss	+ or −	toss	=	0.5
			=	0.5
			=	0.5
			=	0.5
			=	0.5
			=	0.5
			=	0.5

toss	+ or −	toss	=	0.5
			=	0.5
			=	0.5
			=	0.5
			=	0.5
			=	0.5

toss	+ or −	toss	=	0.5
			=	0.5
			=	0.5
			=	0.5
			=	0.5
			=	0.5
			=	0.5

Name ______________________________

Solve.

1	$9 \times 8 =$ ______	**9**	$21 - 11 =$ ______
2	$8 + 4 + 9 =$ ______	**10**	$7 + 6 + 3 =$ ______
3	$16 + 14 =$ ______	**11**	$22 - 7 - 12 =$ ______
4	$24 - 8 =$ ______	**12**	$8 \times 0 =$ ______
5	$6 \times 9 =$ ______	**13**	$15 - 12 + 7 =$ ______
6	$17 - 9 =$ ______	**14**	$17 + 12 =$ ______
7	$3 \times 4 =$ ______	**15**	$20 - 12 =$ ______
8	$4 \times 8 =$ ______		

▶ Fill in the graph to show how many you did correctly in one minute.

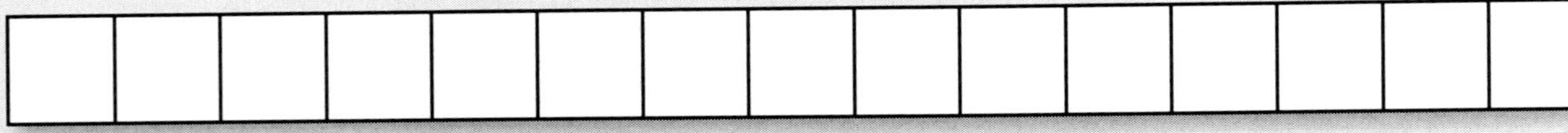

| 1 | 2 | 3 | 4 | 5 | 6 | 7 | 8 | 9 | 10 | 11 | 12 | 13 | 14 | 15 |

My goal for tomorrow is: ______

(Write in the number you want to get correct tomorrow.)

Decimals in Sports

Sport	Event	Record	Comment
Track & Field	100 meter dash [men's]	9.78 seconds	Faster is better
Track & Field	Long Jump	8.95 meters	Higher is better
Track & Field	Pole Vault	6.14 meters	Higher is better
Baseball	Earned-run Average (ERA)	0.96 runs	Lower is better
Basketball	All-Time Best Scoring Average	30.1 points	Higher is better
Swimming	100 meter freestyle	47.84 seconds	Faster is better
Skiing	Team Ski Jumping	974.1 points	Greater is better
Ice Skating	500 meter Speed Skating [women's]	37.3 seconds	Faster is better

Name ___________________________

Circle the least number.

1 0.09 0.11

2 0.90 0.77

3 0.32 0.23

4 0.61 0.59

5 0.19 0.22

6 0.06 0.02

7 0.89 0.90

8 half of 10 = ______

9 half of 6 = ______

10 half of 18 = ______

11 half of 12 = ______

12 quarter of 8 = ______

13 quarter of 16 = ______

14 quarter of 20 = ______

15 quarter of 4 = ______

▶ Fill in the graph to show how many you did correctly in one minute.

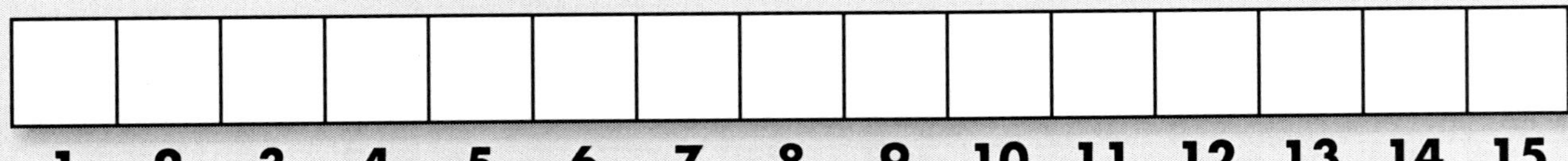

Decimal Number Lines

Name _______________________________

Date _______________________________

1 Write as decimals:

  a $\frac{3}{10}$ = _____   **b** $\frac{68}{100}$ = _____   **c** $\frac{9}{10}$ = _____   **d** $\frac{11}{100}$ = _____

2 Write as fractions:

  a 0.04 = _____   **b** 0.5 = _____   **c** 0.8 = _____   **d** 0.15 = _____

3 Circle the greater number:

  a $\frac{6}{100}$, 0.60   **b** 0.09, 15 out of 100   **c** $\frac{72}{100}$, 59 hundredths

4 Write in order from least to greatest:

  0.21   0.65   0.09   0.81   0.58

  ______   ______   ______   ______   ______

5 On this number line show:

  a $\frac{1}{2}$ on top, 0.5 on the bottom.

  b $\frac{4}{10}$ on top, 0.4 on the bottom.

  c $\frac{9}{10}$ on top, 0.9 on the bottom.

6 Add or subtract.

  a 1.8 + 0.2 = _____   **b** 3.4 + 4.5 = _____   **c** 7.4 − 3.0 = _____

7 Jenny had a fever. Her temperature was 101.8 degrees.
  Which whole degree is nearest to her temperature?

  ○ **a** 100 degrees   ○ **b** 101 degrees   ○ **c** 102 degrees

Name _______________________________

Date _______________________________

8 Write in numerals:
 a three hundred one

 ____

 b five hundred six

 ____

9 Draw lines to show fourths.
 Shade $\frac{1}{2}$.

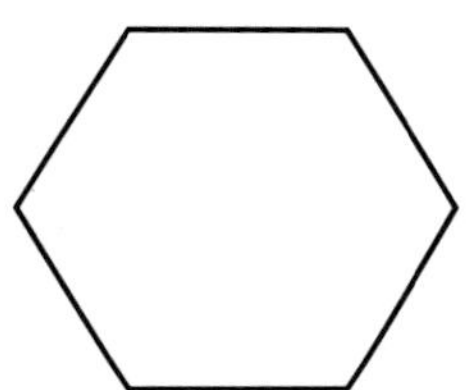

10 a $65 + 19 =$ _______

 b $37 + 23 =$ _______

11
$$\begin{array}{cccc} 6\,7 & \quad 8\,8 & \quad 9\,5 \\ -1\,4 & \quad -3\,5 & \quad -2\,0 \\ \hline \end{array}$$

12 Each chapter in a book has 9 pages. How many pages has Liam read if he's read 8 chapters? _______

13
$$\begin{array}{cccc} 4 & \quad 5 & \quad 7 & \quad 8 \\ \times 1 & \quad \times 3 & \quad \times 9 & \quad \times 6 \\ \hline \end{array}$$

14 Shade to match the fraction.

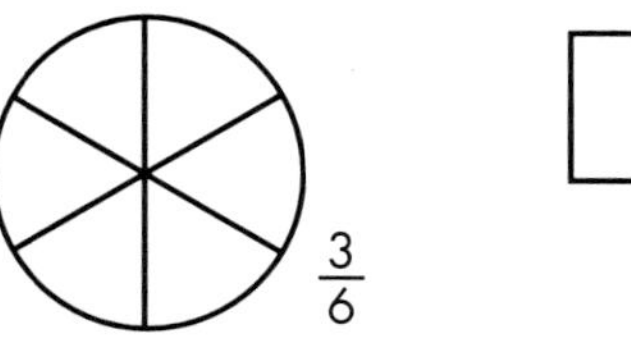

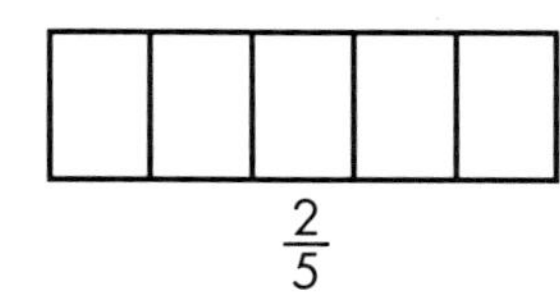

15 What is:
 a $\frac{1}{4}$ of 12 oranges? _______
 b $\frac{1}{3}$ of 15 beans? _______

16 Count backwards by 7s:

 49 _____ _____ _____

17 a $54 \div 6 =$ _______

 b $18 \div 9 =$ _______

18 What number is halfway between 2 and 3? _______

19 Which number is a multiple of 8?
 ◯ **a** 18　◯ **b** 48　◯ **c** 68

20 Chino bought 2 packages of meat from the deli. One weighed 0.8 pounds and the other 0.6 pounds. Did he buy more or less than 1 pound of meat? _______

Improvement Award

ON TARGET

presented to

____

for improvement in

____

Teacher_____________________

Date _______________________

DISTINCTION

____

of class

____

has achieved distinction in the area of

____

Teacher_____________________

Date

Summer Studio Math

Answer Key

Fact Fluency 1
1 39 2 77 3 13 4 50 5 98 6 30 7 60 8 16
9 66 10 25 11 70 12 20 13 61 14 10 15 86

Fact Fluency 2
1 20 2 15 3 20 4 19 5 20 6 25 7 28 8 20
9 35 10 11 11 83 12 24 13 90 14 12 15 15

Fact Fluency 3
1 16 2 11 3 18 4 9 5 14 6 14 7 11 8 12 9 19
10 17 11 15 12 12 13 18 14 14 15 9

Fact Fluency 4
1 142 2 215 3 873 4 529 5 604 6 919 7 450
8 738 9 175, 218, 715 10 97, 258, 301
11 487, 592, 903 12 599, 650, 711 13 182,
281, 812 14 791, 917, 971 15 203, 230, 302

Fact Fluency 5
1 10 2 50 3 10 4 70 5 10 6 40 7 10 8 90
9 10 10 60 11 10 12 80 13 18 14 17 15 19

Fact Fluency 6
1 13 2 9 3 17 4 21 5 7 6 19 7 29 8 39 9 35
10 36 11 31 12 27 13 39 14 38 15 37

Fact Fluency 7
1 27 2 26 3 27 4 29 5 31 6 24 7 28 8 32
9 30 10 28 11 33 12 28 13 28 14 29 15 27

Fact Fluency 8
1 7 2 12 3 7 4 13 5 16 6 7 7 18 8 11 9 16
10 5 11 4 12 19 13 8 14 19 15 10

Fact Fluency 9
1 9 2 8 3 11 4 6 5 9 6 9 7 4 8 7 9 8 10 11
11 3 12 9 13 9 14 7 15 7

Fact Fluency 10
1 35 2 60 3 56 4 52 5 58 6 64 7 37 8 73
9 78 10 54 11 57 12 63 13 41 14 67 15 52

Fact Fluency 11
1 9 2 8 3 11 4 6 5 9 6 9 7 4 8 7 9 8 10 11
11 3 12 9 13 9 14 7 15 7

Fact Fluency 12
1 7 2 12 3 7 4 13 5 16 6 15 7 $4 \times 3 = 12$
8 $5 \times 5 = 25$ 9 $3 \times 7 = 21$ 10 $6 \times 8 = 48$
11 $2 \times 5 = 10$ 12 $4 \times 4 = 16$ 13 $6 \times 3 =$
18 14 $5 \times 10 = 50$ 15 $6 \times 9 = 54$

Fact Fluency 13
1 8 2 15 3 40 4 14 5 10 6 16 7 10 8 12 9 20
10 35 11 50 12 25 13 45 14 30 15 40

Fact Fluency 14
1 16 2 0 3 6 4 28 5 9 6 36 7 72 8 32 9 0 10 0
11 48 12 63 13 0 14 54 15 0

Fact Fluency 15
1 21 2 81 3 48 4 0 5 24 6 80 7 24 8 9 9 54
10 42 11 72 12 32 13 36 14 40 15 7

Fact Fluency 16
1 20 2 0 3 11 4 13 5 42 6 4 7 8 8 30 9 21
10 9 11 11 12 64 13 100 14 24 15 1

Fact Fluency 17
1 4 2 9 3 6 4 4 5 6 6 3 7 7 8 6 9 7 10 7 11 9
12 3 13 4 14 3 15 8

Fact Fluency 18
1 $8 \times 7 = 56$ 2 $56 \div 8 = 7$ 3 $56 \div 7 = 8$
4 $4 \times 9 = 36$ 5 $36 \div 9 = 4$ 6 $36 \div 4 = 9$
7 $9 \times 6 = 54$ 8 $54 \div 9 = 6$ 9 $54 \div 6 = 9$
10 $48 \div 8 = 6$ 11 $6 \times 8 = 48$ 12 $8 \times 6 =$
48 13 $63 \div 9 = 7$ 14 $9 \times 7 = 63$ 15 $7 \times$
$9 = 63$

Fact Fluency 19
1 36 2 9 3 72 4 8 5 42 6 8 7 0 8 8 9 48 10 49
11 36 12 9 13 27 14 3 15 49

Fact Fluency 20
1 6 2 10 3 6 4 8 5 7 6 4 7 8 8 9 9 4 10 3
11 10 12 7 13 3 14 5 15 5

Fact Fluency 21
1 16 2 35 3 24 4 90 5 32 6 0 7 313 8 549
9 351 10 11 11 9 12 13 13 13 14 19 15 57

Fact Fluency 22
1 27 2 93 3 42 4 55 5 63 6 77 7 81 8 19 9 32 10 8
11 64 12 4 13 49 14 8 15 0

Fact Fluency 23
1 82 2 15 3 30 4 16 5 21 6 5 7 20 8 49 2 10 3
11 6 12 6 13 9 14 10 15 25

Fact Fluency 24
1 $\frac{1}{2}$ 2 $\frac{1}{2}$ 3 $\frac{3}{4}$ 4 $\frac{2}{8}$ 5 $\frac{2}{6}$ 6 $\frac{3}{8}$ 7 $\frac{3}{5}$ 8 $\frac{4}{5}$ 9 > 10 =
11 < 12 > 13 > 14 = 15 >

Fact Fluency 25
1–5: Complete a sample to go over with
students 6 10 7 4 8 7 9–12: Complete a
sample to go over with students
13 25 14 10 15 12

Fact Fluency 26
1 339 2 713 3 209 4 650 5 1,256 6 7,199
7 8,719 8 3,330 9 302 10 989 11 2,692
12 4,190 13 8,223 14 5,703 15 2,399

Fact Fluency 27
1 8 2 6 3 2 4 650 5 307 6 806 7 38 8 101
9 200 10 503 11 119 12 195, 205, 302
13 200+70+3 14 900+10+8 15
600+0+5

Fact Fluency 28
1 0.09 2 0.77 3 0.23 4 0.59 5 0.19 6 0.02
7 0.89 8 5 9 3 10 9 11 6 12 2 13 4 14 5 15 1

Fact Fluency 29
1 $\frac{1}{4}$ 2 0.50 3 0.90 4 $\frac{100}{100}$ 5 0.07 6 $\frac{3}{4}$ 7 $\frac{32}{100}$
8 0.85 9 < 10 = 11 = 12 > 13 > 14 = 15 >

Fact Fluency 30
1 72 2 21 3 30 4 16 5 54 6 8 7 12 8 32 9 10
10 16 11 3 12 0 13 10 14 29 15 8

Day 1
1a 3 b 1 c 2 d 6 e 4 f 7 g 5 h 8 2a 12 b 12 c 15 d 17 3a $14 b $13 c $8
d $12

Day 2
1a 200 + 40 + 3 = 243; b 4 hundreds 3 tens 7 ones 400 + 30 +
7 = 437; c 1 hundred 6 tens 5 ones 100 + 60 + 5 = 165
d 6 hundreds 4 tens 0 ones 600 + 40 + 0 = 640; 2a 312 b 867
c 501 d 301 e 641 f 221 g 550 h 900; 3 529, 599, 601, 655

Day 3
1a 240 b 143 c 319; 2a 300 + 50 + 6 b 700 + 20 + 4 c 400 + 30 +
1 d 100 + 60 + 8; e 900 + 40 + 2 f 600 + 0 + 5 g 200 + 20 +
0 h 800 + 10 + 1; 3a 235 b 900 c 710 d 102 e 419 f 821 ; 4a six
hundred twelve b nine hundred fifty; c three hundred forty-eight

Day 4
1a less than b more than c more than d less than
2a more than b less than c more than d more than
3a less than b less than c more than d less than
4a cross out 185, 315 b cross out 80, 100
c cross out 2,100, 2,350 d cross out 850, 900
5 16 + 18 > 30; There will not be enough seats.

Day 5
1a 10 b 10 c 30 d 30 e 40 f 60 g 70 h 70 i 90 j 100
2a 53, 51, 54, 52 b 58, 56, 55, 59
3a 94, 91, 93, 92 b 97, 95, 102, 99
4a 728, 713, 749, 706 b 761, 783, 790, 755
5a 20 b 20 c 90 d 80; 80 beads

Day 1
1a 11 **b** 14 **c** 20 **d** 20 **e** 19 **f** 17 **g** 16 **h** 14 **i** 19 **2a** 8 + 8 = 16
b 5 + 5 = 10 **c** 9 + 9 = 18 **d** 16 + 16 = 32 **3a** 9 **b** 9 + 9 + 1 = 19
4a 88 **b** 99 **c** 69 **d** 75

Day 2
1a 15 feet **b** 11 inches **2a** 15 − 4 = 11 **b** 18 − 6 = 12

Day 3
1a 8 **b** 7 **c** 12 **d** 8 **e** 17 **f** 12 **g** 6 **h** 6 **i** 18

2b 4; 40; 400 **c** 3; 50 − 20 = 30; 500 − 200 = 300; **d** 2; 80 − 60
= 20; 800 − 600 = 200; **3a** 44 **b** 42 **c** 15 **d** 22

Day 4
1a 34 + 47 = 81 **b** 28 + 54 = 82 **c** 39 + 60 = 99 **d** 65 + 54 =
119; **2** 218 **3** 713 **4** 902

Day 5
1a 34 **b** 18 **c** 27 **d** 13 **e** 28 **f** 18 **2** 39 **3** 166 **4** 273

Day 1
1a 24 **b** 36 **c** 15 **d** 7 **2a** 3 **b** 4 **c** 12 **d** 12 **3a** 6 **b** 3 **c** 18 **d** 18

Day 2
A 1 × 24; 2 × 12; 3 × 8; 4 × 6; 6 × 4; 8 × 3; 12 × 2; 24 × 1
B 1 × 18; 2 × 9; 3 × 6; 6 × 3; 9 × 2; 18 × 1; **C** 1 × 36; 2 × 18;
3 × 12; 4 × 9; 6 × 6; 9 × 4; 12 × 3; 18 × 2; 36 × 1; **D** 1 × 12;
2 × 6; 3 × 4; 4 × 3; 6 × 2; 12 × 1; **problem:** 28

Day 3
1a 6 **b** 42 **c** 18 **d** 60 **e** 0 **f** 0 **2a** 6 **b** 0 **c** 0 **d** 9 **e** 0 **f** 0; **3** 18, 24, 30, 36,
42, 48, 54, 60 **4** 10 × 8 = 80; 2 × 8 = 16; 5 × 8 = 40; 8 × 8 =
64; 0 × 8 = 0; 1 × 8 = 8; 6 × 8 = 48; 4 × 8 = 32; 9 × 8 = 72;
3 × 8 = 24; 7 × 8 = 56

Day 4
1a 24, 20, 16, 12, 8, 4 **b** 18, 16, 14, 12, 10, 8 **c** 25, 20, 15, 10, 5, 0
d 90, 80, 70, 60, 50, 40 **2a** 32; 12 **b** 18; 10 **c** 30; 40 **d** 10; 20 **e** 20;
45 **f** 28; 16; **3a** 9; 0; 15; 21; 27; 18; 24; 6; 12; 30 **b** 0; 25; 45; 30;
10; 50; 20; 35; 15; 40; **c** 70; 50; 10; 80; 40; 100; 0; 60; 20; 90

Day 5
1a 7; 14; 21; 28; 35; 42; 49; 56; 63; 70; 77; 84; 91; 98; **b** 8; 16; 24;
32; 40; 48; 56; 64; 72; 80; 88; 96; **c** 9; 18; 27; 36; 45; 54; 63; 72;
81; 90; 99; **d** 56 is a multiple of 7 and 8; 63 is a multiple of 7 and
9; 72 is a multiple of 8 and 9

Day 1
1a 4 groups; 12 hearts **b** 6 groups; 12 hearts **2a** 8 **b** 6 **3** 4

Day 2
A 4 × 6 = 24; 6 × 4 = 24; 24 ÷ 4 = 6; 24 ÷ 6 = 4
B 4 × 10 = 40; 10 × 4 = 40; 40 ÷ 4 = 10; 40 ÷ 10 = 4
C 2 × 12 = 24; 12 × 2 = 24; 24 ÷ 2 = 12; 24 ÷ 12 = 2
D 2 × 9 = 18; 9 × 2 = 18; 18 ÷ 2 = 9; 18 ÷ 9 = 2
E 1 × 7 = 7; 7 × 1 = 7; 7 ÷ 1 = 7; 7 ÷ 7 = 1

Day 3
1a 9 R0 **b** 8 R0 **c** 2 R0 **d** 10 R0 **e** 5 R1 **f** 6 R6 **g** 6 R4 **h** 2 R4 **i** 10 R0
j remainder **Problem:** 4 books; 6 boxes

Day 4
1a 3 **b** 4 **c** 8 **d** 1 **e** 6 **f** 24 **2a** 3 **b** 5 **c** 10 **d** 6 **e** 1 **f** 30
3a 30; 6; 5 **b** 18; 6; 3 **c** 32; 8; 4 **4a** 6 **b** 2 **c** 2 **d** 3 **e** 6 **f** 7
5a 30 ÷ 6 = 5 **b** 48 ÷ 4 = 12 **c** 600 ÷ 100 = 6

Day 5
1b 9)54 = 6 **c** 9)27 = 3 **d** 9)72 = 8 **2a** 6)36 = 6 **b** 6)48 = 8 **c** 6)18 = 3
d 6)42 = 7 **3a** 8)56 = 7 **b** 8)24 = 3 **c** 8)64 = 8 **d** 8)32 = 4

Day 1
1a–f: Complete a sample to go over with students
d seventh **e** ninth **f** fourth
2a one **b** one **c** one **d** one tenth **e** one ninth **f** one sixth

Day 2
1a 2 **b** 5 **c** 8 **d** 10 **2a** 2 **b** 5 **c** 2 **d** 2 **3a** T **b** F **c** F **d** F **4** Answer will vary

Day 3
1a 5 **b** 7 **c** 8 **2a** 2 **b** 3 **c** 4 **3a** 1 **b** 2 **c** 3; **4a** 2 bananas **b** 3 cherries
c 6 apples **Problem:** 3; 6

Day 4

Problem: $\frac{3}{8}$

Day 5
1a 1$\frac{1}{2}$ in. **b** $\frac{1}{2}$ in. **c** 3 in. **d** 4$\frac{1}{2}$ in. **e** 4 in. **2a-d** Complete a
sample to go over with students.

Day 1
1a 50 moons **b** 10 moons **c** 25 moons **d** $\frac{50}{100}$; 0.50; **e** $\frac{25}{100}$; 0.25
f $\frac{10}{100}$; 0.10 **g** $\frac{75}{100}$; 0.75 **h** $\frac{100}{100}$; 1.0; **2a** $\frac{50}{100}$; 0.50; $\frac{1}{2}$ **b** $\frac{25}{100}$; 0.25; $\frac{1}{4}$
c $\frac{100}{100}$; 1; 1; **d** $\frac{50}{100}$; 0.50; $\frac{1}{2}$ **e** $\frac{50}{100}$; 0.50; $\frac{1}{2}$

Day 2
1a $\frac{2}{10}$ = 0.2 **b** $\frac{4}{10}$ = 0.4 **c** $\frac{6}{10}$ = 0.6; **2a** 1 column **b** 8 columns
c 3 columns **d** 9 columns; **3a** C **b** A **c** D **d** B **e** D **f** B **g** E **h** C

Day 3
1a E **b** D **c** G **d** A **e** B **f** H **g** C **h** F **2a** A **b** H **c** D **3a** B **b** E **c** G
Problem: Jacob

Day 4
a 10.5 **b** 10.9 **c** 9.6 **d** 4.8 **e** 9.7 **f** 6.8 **g** 8.5 **h** 7.86 **i** 6.29
j 9.59 **k** 5.13 **l** 5.31 **m** 5.52 **n** 1.15 **o** 4.52 **Problem:** 1.5 miles

Day 5
1a 1 **b** 4 **c** 6 **d** 1 **e** 7 **f** 3 **g** 10 **h** 4 **i** 63 **j** 13 **k** 19 **l** 30
2a $2 **b** $2 **c** $6 **d** $3 **e** $8 **f** $3 **g** $8 **h** $3 **i** $2
3
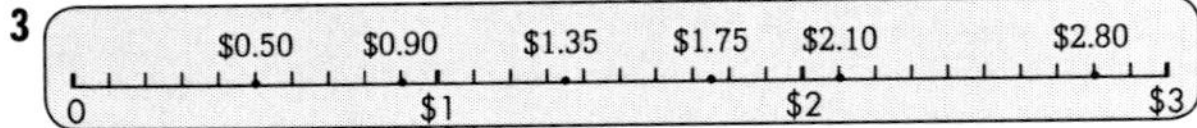

4 $6, $5, Juan, $1

---

148   Summer Studio Math

Pre Test

1a 0.4 **b** 0.39 **c** 0.7 **d** 0.56 **2a** $\frac{12}{100}$ **b** $\frac{6}{10}$ **c** $\frac{98}{100}$ **d** $\frac{85}{100}$ **3a** 0.40 **b** 8 out of 100 **c** $\frac{68}{100}$
4 0.06, 0.17, 0.25, 0.49, 0.98

5 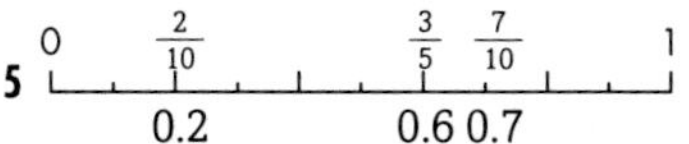

6a 3.7 **b** 9.7 **c** 4.1 **7** B **8a** 430 **b** 612
9 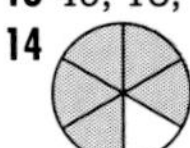 **10** 65 **11** 52; 42; 79 **12** $24
13 40; 18; 14; 45
14 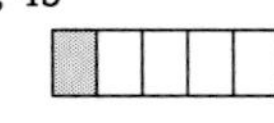

15a 2 **b** 5 **16** 35, 30, 25 **17a** 6 **b** 2 **18** 1.5
19 Less than 1 pound

Assessment 1

1a 235 **b** 109 **2** 212, 673, 704, 754 **3** C
4a 46 **b** 219 **5a** 11 **b** 12 **c** 10 **6a** 30 **b** 10 **c** 90
7 A

Assessment 2

1a 17 **b** 62 **c** 72 **d** 16 **e** 79 **f** 9 **g** 55 **h** 18
i 7 **2a** 217 **b** 148 **3** B

Cumulative Assessment 3

1a 6 **b** 6 **c** 36 **d** 6 + 6 + 6 + 6 + 6 + 6 =
36 **e** 6 × 6 = 36 **2** 3 × 5 = 15; 5 × 3 =
15 **3a** 0 **b** 9 **c** 2 **d** 0 **e** 30 **f** 12 **g** 63 **h** 16 **4a** 30,
24, 18, 12, 6 **b** 32, 24, 16, 8, 0 **c** 40 **5a** 371
b 506 **c** 240 **6a** 125 **b** 710 **5** C **6a** 308 **b** 475
7 309, 319, 331, 380, 390, 399 **8a** 36 **b** 318
9a 60 **b** 26 **c** 214 **d** 138 **10** 22 inches **11** A

Assessment 4

1a 9 **b** 6 **c** 18 **2** 5; 5; 5 **3a** 54; 9; 6 **b** 42; 6; 7
4a 8 **b** 7 **c** 9 **5a** 6 R1 **c** 3 R2 **d** 6 R2 **6** C

Assessment 5

1 c, e **2** 5 bars; 4 keys; 8 cars **3a** 2 **b** 4 **c** 5
d 10 **4a** 6 **b** 8 **c** 4 **d** 9 **5** B

Cumulative Assessment 6

1a 0.3 **b** 0.68 **c** 0.9 **d** 0.11 **2a** $\frac{4}{100}$ **b** $\frac{5}{10}$ **c** $\frac{8}{10}$ **d** $\frac{15}{100}$ **3a** 0.60 **b** 15 out of 100 **c** $\frac{72}{100}$
4 0.09, 0.21, 0.58, 0.65, 0.81

5 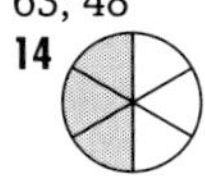

6a 2.0 **b** 7.9 **c** 4.4 **7** C

8a 301 **b** 506 **9** 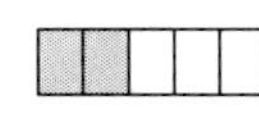
10 84 **b** 60 **11** 53; 53; 75 **12** 72 **13** 4; 15;
63; 48
14

15a 3 **b** 5 **16** 42, 35, 28 **17a** 9 **b** 9 **18** 2.5 **19** B
20 More than 1 pound

Answers provided where appropriate.

BLM 13

a 3 + 3 + 3 = 9; 3 × 3 = 9 **b** 5 + 5 + 5 +
5 = 20; 4 × 5 = 20 **c** 1 + 1 + 1 + 1 + 1
+ 1 + 1 = 7; 7 × 1 = 7 **d** 6 + 6 + 6 + 6
+ 6 + 6 + 6 = 42; 7 × 6 = 42 **e** 2 + 2 +
2 + 2 + 2 + 2 + 2 + 2 + 2 + 2 = 20; 10
× 2 = 20 **f** 4 + 4 + 4 + 4 + 4 + 4 + 4
= 28; 7 × 4 = 28 **g** 1 = 1; 1 × 1 = 1

BLM 17

1 3 × 2 = 6; 2 × 3 = 6 **2** 4 × 2 = 8; 2 ×
4 = 8 **3** 2 × 6 = 12; 6 × 2 = 12 **4** 3 × 5
= 15; 5 × 3 = 15 **5** 4 × 3 = 12; 3 × 4 =
12 **6** 2 × 5 = 10; 5 × 2 = 10

Draw a diagram: 1 × 24; 2 × 12; 3 × 8; 4 ×
6; 6 × 4; 8 × 3; 12 × 2; 24 × 1; 8 arrays

BLM 19

1a 8 × 4 = 32 **b** 6 × 6 = 36 **c** 3 × 7 = 21
2a 8 × 4 = 32 **b** 6 × 8 = 48 **3** 6 × 3 = 18;
8 × 4 = 32; 7 × 5 = 35; 9 × 9 = 81; 4 ×
1 = 4; 8 × 6 = 48

BLM 20

Any factor multiplied by zero has a
product of zero. Any factor multiplied by
one has a product equal to that factor.
Factors multiplied in a different order
will have the same product.

BLM 28

1 24 **2a** 6 **b** 8 **c** 2 **d** 1 **3** 12 **4** 4 each; 4 left
over

BLM 36

1 $\frac{1}{2}$ **2** $\frac{3}{4}$ **3** $\frac{1}{4}$ **4** $\frac{2}{3}$ **5** $\frac{1}{8}$ **6** $\frac{1}{4}$
7-9: Complete a sample to go over with
students

Answers provided where appropriate

Activity Card 301

180, 210, 340, 370, 650, 690, 730, 760, 850, 920

Activity Card 302

7, 3, 8
Least: 378 (three hundred seventy-eight)
Greatest: 873 (eight hundred seventy-three)
6, 0, 4
Least: 406 (four hundred six)
Greatest: 640 (six hundred forty)
0, 8, 6
Least: 608 (six hundred eight)
Greatest: 860 (eight hundred sixty)
2, 5, 9
Least: 259 (two hundred fifty nine)
Greatest: 952 (nine hundred fifty two)

Activity Card 306

7, 1, 3: 71, 73, 17, 13, 37, 31, 713, 731, 173, 137, 371, 317, 12
numbers; 0, 5, 8: 58, 50, 85, 80, 508, 580, 805, 850, 8 numbers;
not as many

Activity Card 309

708: seven hundred eight
540: five hundred forty
217: two hundred seventeen
683: six hundred eighty-three
499: four hundred ninety-nine
536: five hundred thirty-six
271: two hundred seventy-one
Least to greatest: 217, 271, 499, 536, 540, 683, 708
Rounded: 200; 300; 500; 500; 500; 700; 700

Activity Card 311

banana, apple   banana, orange   apple, orange

Activity Card 315

86 − 24 = 62; 86 − 40 = 46; 86 − 33 = 53; 57 − 24 = 33;
57 − 40 = 17; 57 − 33 = 24; 95 − 24 = 71; 95 − 40 = 55;
95 − 33 = 62 Least to greatest: 17, 24, 33, 46, 53, 55, 62, 62, 71

Activity Card 316

31 − 15 = 16; 87 − 15 − 72; 99 − 15 = 84; 54 − 15 = 39;
29 − 15 = 14; 75 − 15 = 60; 26 − 15 = 11; 66 − 15 = 51

Activity Card 318

62 + 33; 26 + 69; 29 + 66; 71 + 24; 1 + 94; 17 + 78; 47 + 48;
80 + 15; 55 + 40

Activity Card 320

38 − 17 = 21; 77 − 53 = 24; 23 − 10 = 13; 55 − 41 = 14;

38 − 23 = 15; 77 − 55 = 22; 17 − 10 = 7; 53 − 41 = 12

Activity Card 321
49 − 17 = 32; 49 − 26 = 23; 49 − 35 = 14; 68 − 17 = 51;
68 − 26 = 42; 68 − 35 = 33; 87 − 17 = 70; 87 − 26 = 61;
87 − 35 = 52; Greatest to least: 70, 61, 52, 51, 42, 33, 32, 23, 14

Activity Card 325
10 − 5 = 5; 20 + 5 = 25; 45 − 5 = 40; 65 + 5 = 70;
60 − 5 = 55; 30 + 5 = 35; 70 − 5 = 55; 10 + 5 = 15;
100 − 5 = 95; 95 + 5 = 100; 80 − 5 = 75; 40 + 5 = 45;
35 − 5 = 30; 80 + 5 = 85; 90 − 5 = 85; 55 + 5 = 60;
15 − 5 = 10; 45 + 5 = 50; 20 − 5 =15; 5 + 5 = 10

Activity Card 326
Greatest: 276 + 8 and 278 + 6; Least: 2 + 7 + 6 + 8

Activity Card 328
65 + 69; 66 + 68; 130 + 4; 107 + 27; 47 + 87;
119 + 15; 72 + 62; 59 + 75; 13 + 121; 99 + 35

Activity Card 329
candles: 8; 12; 16; 20; toes: 20; 30; 40; 50;
wheels: 8; 12; 16; 20; eyes: 4; 6; 8; 10;

Activity Card 330
Olga: 30; Cathy: 20; Emma: 80; Tonya: 40; José: 70; Oldest:
Emma; 80

Activity Card 334
Mo: 15, 30; Bo: 12, 15, 18, 24, 30; Jo: 12, 24
Po: 12, 18, 24, 30; Lo: 18

Activity Card 335
6 × 4 = 24; 8 × 6 = 48; 30 × 4 = 120; 4 × 6 = 24; 7 × 4 = 28;
1 × 6 = 6; 50 × 4 = 200; 9 × 6 = 54; 20 × 4 = 80; 50 × 6 =
300; 8 × 4 = 32; 3 × 6 = 18; 1 × 4 = 4; 100 × 6 = 600; 0 × 4 =
0; 7 × 6 = 42 9 × 4 = 36; 6 × 6 = 36; 3 × 4 = 12; 2 × 6 = 12
100 × 4 = 400; 80 × 6 = 480; 40 × 4 = 160; 0 × 6 = 0

Activity Card 339
48 × 1; 24 × 2; 16 × 3; 12 × 4; 6 × 8;
8 × 6; 4 × 12; 3 × 16; 2 × 24; 1 × 48

Activity Card 340
96 × 1; 48 × 2; 32 × 3; 24 × 4; 13 × 6; 12 × 8; 6 pairs of factors
144 × 1; 72 × 2; 48 × 3; 36 × 4; 24 × 6; 18 × 8; 16 × 9; 12 ×
12; 8 pairs of factors

Activity Card 341
6 = 2 × 3; 20 = 4 × 5; 56 = 7 × 8; 90 = 9 × 10; 12 = 3 × 4;
30 = 5 × 6; 42 = 6 × 7

Activity Card 342
4 × 6 = 24; 4 × 5 = 20; 4 × 9 = 36; 4 × 7 = 28; 6 × 6 = 36;
6 × 5 = 30; 6 × 9 = 54; 6 × 7 = 42; 8 × 6 = 48; 8 × 5 = 40;
8 × 9 = 72; 8 × 7 = 56; 7 × 6 = 42; 7 × 5 = 35; 7 × 9 = 63;
7 × 7 = 49; 9 × 6 = 54; 9 × 5 = 45; 9 × 9 = 81; 9 × 7 = 63

Activity Card 343
45 is 9 groups of 5; 18 is 3 groups of 6; 18 is 6 groups of 3
40 is 8 groups of 5; 40 is 5 groups of 8; 40 is 10 groups of 4
40 is 4 groups of 10; 72 is 9 groups of 8; 72 is 8 groups of 9
54 is 9 groups of 6; 54 is 6 groups of 9; 21 is 3 groups of 7
21 is 7 groups of 3; 36 is 9 groups of 4; 36 is 4 groups of 9
36 is 6 groups of 6; g is 1 group of 6; 6 is 6 groups of 1

Activity Card 344
43 ÷ 6 = 7 R1; 43 ÷ 5 = 8 R3; 43 ÷ 9 = 4 R7; 43 ÷ 7 = 6 R1;
62 ÷ 6 = 10 R2; 62 ÷ 5 = 12 R2; 62 ÷ 9 = 6 R8; 62 ÷ 7 = 8 R8;
84 ÷ 6 = 14; 84 ÷ 5 = 16 R4; 84 ÷ 9 = 9 R3; 84 ÷ 7 = 12;
75 ÷ 6 = 12 R3; 75 ÷ 5 = 15; 75 ÷ 9 = 8 R3; 75 ÷ 7 = 10 R5;
98 ÷ 6 = 16 R2; 98 ÷ 5 = 19 R3; 98 ÷ 9 = 10 8; 98 ÷ 7 = 14

Activity Card 345
36:1 group of 36; 2 groups of 18; 3 groups of 12;

4 groups of 9; 6 groups of 6; 9 groups of 4;
12 groups of 3; 18 groups of 2; 36 groups of 1
20: 1 group of 20; 2 groups of 10; 4 groups of 5;
5 groups of 4; 10 groups of 2; 20 groups of 1

Activity Card 348
5: 10, 25, 30, 35, 45; 4: 8, 12, 16, 28, 32, 36, 48
6: 12, 18, 30, 36, 42, 48; 9: 18, 36, 45, 63, 81

Activity Card 350
80 ÷ 10 = 8; 72 ÷ 9 = 8; 64 ÷ 8 = 8; 56 ÷ 7 = 8; 48 ÷ 6 = 8; 40
÷ 5 = 8; 32 ÷ 4 = 8; 24 ÷ 3 = 8; 16 ÷ 2 = 8; 8 ÷ 1 = 8; 60 ÷ 10
= 6; 54 ÷ 9 = 6; 48 ÷ 8 = 6; 42 ÷ 7 = 6; 36 ÷ 6 = 6; 30 ÷ 5 =
6; 24 ÷ 4 = 6; 18 ÷ 3 = 6; 12 ÷ 2 = 6; 6 ÷ 1 = 6; 90 ÷ 10 = 9;
81 ÷ 9 = 9; 72 ÷ 8 = 9; 63 ÷ 7 = 9; 54 ÷ 6 = 9; 45 ÷ 5 = 9; 36 ÷
4 = 9; 27 ÷ 3 = 9; 18 ÷ 2 = 9; 9 ÷ 1 = 9

Activity Card 351
3

Activity Card 354
0 ÷ 4 = 0; 32 ÷ 4 = 8; 16 ÷ 4 = 4; 40 ÷ 4 = 10; 12 ÷ 4 = 3;
4 ÷ 4 = 1; 28 ÷ 4 = 7; 20 ÷ 4 = 5; 8 ÷ 4 = 2; 36 ÷ 4 = 9; 24 ÷
4 = 6

Activity Card 355
Hilly: 6; Marvin: 15; Molly: 48; Molly has the most

Activity Card 356
2 ÷ 11 = 0.181818181818; 3 ÷ 11 = 0.272727272727;
4 ÷ 11 = 0.363636363636; 5 ÷ 11 = 0.454545454545;
6 ÷ 11 = 0.545454545454; 7 ÷ 11 = 0.636363636363;
8 ÷ 11 = 0.727272727272; 9 ÷ 11 = 0.818181818181;
The repeating decimal is the dividend times nine.

Activity Card 357

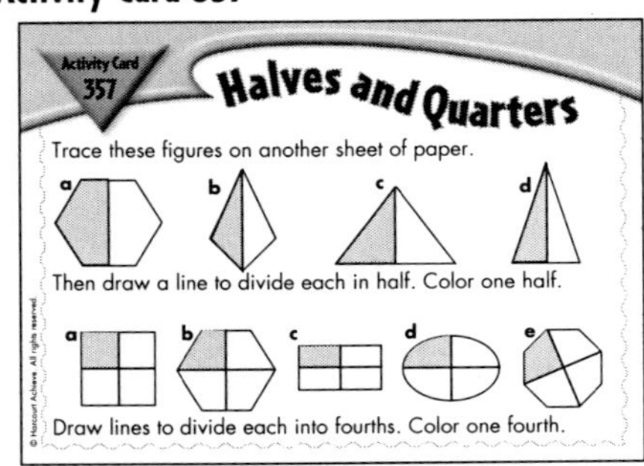

Activity Card 359
1 one 2 one 3 one 4 one 5 one third
6 one tenth 7 one eighth 8 one fifth

Activity Card 360
1 D,G 2 B, E, I, F 3 C, H 4 A 5 ½ 6 ¼

Activity Card 362
One eighth has no topping.

Activity Card 364

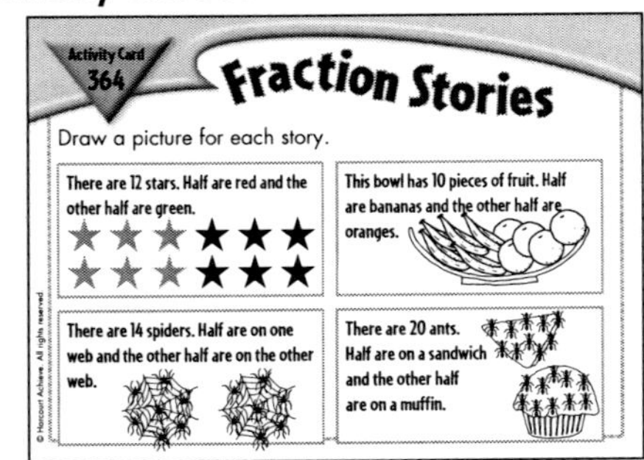

Activity Card 365

Activity Card 366

$\frac{2}{4} > \frac{2}{8}$, $\frac{3}{4} > \frac{1}{2}$

Activity Card 367

1 STAND **2** PEG **3** RING **4** CLOUD

Activity Card 368

5 horses; 10 cows

Activity Card 369

A $3\frac{1}{2}$ **B** 2 **C** $2\frac{1}{2}$ **D** 5 **E** $1\frac{1}{2}$ **F** $3\frac{1}{2}$

Activity Card 371

4a 20 **b** 0.20

Activity Card 373

1 4.6 **2** 0.63 **3** 1.19 **4** 2.7 **5** 3.09 **6** 6.48 **7** 5.1

Activity Card 374

1b $0.73 **c** $0.94 **d** $0.28 **e** $0.19 **f** $0.40
2a 82¢ **b** 95¢ **c** 17¢ **d** 74¢ **e** 49¢ **f** 10¢

Activity Card 376

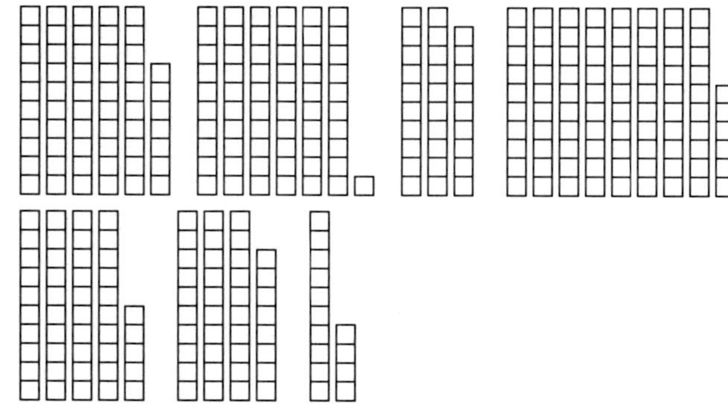

Activity Card 379

1 2.62, 2.77, 2.92, 3.07 **2** 9.77, 9.66, 9.55, 9.44
3 41.04, 39.44, 37.84, 36.44

Activity Card 380

1 0.6 **2** 0.7 **3** 0.66 **4** 0.95 **5** 0.25

Activity Card 381

a 4 **b** 8 **c** 12 **d** 16
e 0.04   0.08   0.12   0.16
f Each term is 0.04 more than the previous term
g Next term: 0.20

Activity Card 383

a $1.23 + $4.64 = $5.87 **b** $0.65 + $3.24 = $3.89
c $1.32 + $0.65 = $1.97 **d** $4.64 + $3.24 = $7.88
e $1.23 + $0.65 = $1.88

Activity Card 384

10; blue and red
